THE ULTIMATE CARE GUIDE FOR CALICO CAT OWNERS:

EVERYTHING YOU NEED TO KNOW TO TRAIN, PROTECT & KEEP YOUR PET HEALTHY & HAPPY

Table of Contents

THE CHARACTERISTICS
OF A CALICO CAT

Calico cats are also known by the name Torties, because of their tortoise shell markings on their coat. Calico cats are considered a lucky breed of cat in many places of the world today.

Calico cats have a life expectancy of about 15 years on average, some a little more, some a little less. They are not a defined breed of cat, but they are a combination of color patterns that make them look the way they look.

The existence of patches in Calico cats was traced back to the importation of domesticated cats along trade routes in Europe and Northern Africa areas. Genetically Calico cats are tortoise shell cats in every way, except that they have a white spot gene on them.

The word "Calico " comes from a cloth imported into Britain from India. The cloth was called "Calicut" and the British people changed the pronunciation to "Calico " when referring to the tri-colored cats that resembled the imported, brightly printed cloth they liked. The word "Calico " represents the color pattern of a white cat with orange and black patches on its coat and these cats come in all shapes and sizes.

Studies show that the Calico cats came about around the time period of 1948. Calico cats are almost always female. This is because the X chromosome determines the color of the cat, and this cat is defined by their colors. Females have two X chromosomes, so one X chromosome will have the orange gene and the other will have the black gene.

It is very possible for a male cat to have tortoise markings. The male Calico cat has a rare condition which is called Klinefelter's Syndrome, this syndrome alters the chromosomes. Sadly, male Calico s may have other genetic changes besides the color of their coat that could affect their health as well. Since Calico is a color pattern and not an actual breed of cat, there isn't an average size, since cats come in so many shapes and sizes.

HOW TO POTTY TRAIN YOUR CAT

Did you ever dream that your favorite and adorable precious cat would do his poo in your human toilet and not in the cat litter box? You might have seen this kind of act in the movies and on TV, but you wonder how exactly this could be done. Aren't cats stubborn creatures, with a mind of their own? Can they actually be potty trained? There is a way to do it, but you have to have loads of patience.

The first thing is, if at all possible, dedicate a toilet, and yes a real toilet for your cat.

The second thing to do is very simple and logical. Just take the cat litter box and place it next to the toilet. Leave it there for a day or so. Let your cat get used to the idea that her litter box and the toilet are close to each other and non-threatening to one another.

Next, raise the level of the litter box from the floor. Do this a little bit at a time by placing thick books like phone books if you have some, to put under it. Do not substitute a box for the books, not yet anyway. This is because a box is naturally taller than a couple of books. You do not want to create a new and unfamiliar situation. The rise in the height of the box from the floor must be very, very small each time. Do not threaten your cat unnecessarily by changing the box's height abruptly. Do it as gradually as possible. Patience is the best way you are going to get your cat to do this for you.

As the litter box's height increases, take off a bit of litter from the box. Again, do this gradually. This is because you do not want to create anything unfamiliar to your cat.

After a few days, the height of the box should now be close to the height of the toilet. And if all is right, your cat will do her stuff in her box, as usual. Take care to ensure that the box is secure, because as its height increases, it may fall when your cat jumps onto it, and will mess the whole process up.

Now, move the box nearer to the toilet seat. Gradually that is, until it is about one inch into the toilet seat, and later, directly over the seat. By this time, the amount of litter in the box should be very, very little.

At this point, your cat should already have the idea that she should urinate and defecate in the toilet area. The real transition now begins, where you use a 'training toilet' and keep decreasing the amount of litter in the box.

Specifically built commercial cat potty training devices can help you at this stage of the training. Each comes with instructions, which you must follow closely. You must always pay attention to your cat's safety, because in doing this and if the training toilet is not placed securely, your cat might fall into the toilet bowl.

There will come the 'moment of truth' when you finally remove the training toilet altogether. If you carry out the training well, your cat can figure out what to do next.

The whole process is a slow one, and all the while you might be wondering if your cat will ever get it. That is a valid concern, but you really do not have much to lose, other than a bit of your time in the weeks that this training is carried out, and it's a pretty cool trick to show your guests!

ITEMS YOU SHOULD NEVER LET YOUR CAT EAT

Although cats may seem to be more resilient than dogs, where their digestive processes are concerned they are approximately about the same. A cat reacts much the same to some foods as dogs and often the reaction may be fatal. As with aspirin or Valium pills, they can kill your pet very quickly and painfully, so if you think your dog or cat has a headache or they are very agitated the best thing is to take them to a vet and have the problem looked at.

Medications for animals may sound very similar to one you yourself take, but they do not contain all the substances the human drug does and far less of anything pain either relief or antibiotic.

Humans often are on diets, of which tuna is a major food for the human, but it is not the same as the tuna your cat eats, and your cat will suffer malnutrition should you decide to feed her what you yourself are eating. The human tuna does not have the vitamins and minerals that your cat needs to help his and her bones and body remain healthy, and therefore he or she will suffer slow starvation.

We are always told not to feed cat's onions or garlic because of a substance in these, which damages the nervous system. Well, this includes baby food, the little snack that your pet can grab from under the high chair can build up in their system and give your cat problems. Some baby foods have onion or garlic salt added to give the food flavor and this will build up in the animal's body and possibly poison it.

You may enjoy a drink of alcohol after work or at a party, but it is not wise to see how drunk your animal can get by deliberately feeding it alcohol. Horses, elephants, and cows can drink some alcohol without too much problems, but because they are so much smaller in body mass than we are as a rule, cats cannot handle it at all, and excrete it very slowly. All the while, their brain and nervous system are receiving irreparable damage as well as other vital organs. Too much alcohol can kill a cat very painfully, so never let your cat near the alcohol.

Many of us like to bake and the baking powder or soda we use is also not at all good for our cats. Try not to let them lick any of the spilled substance up as it can behave very badly with their electrolytes and other body fluids, such as urine. It can also cause congestive heart failure or severe muscle spasms.

HOW TO TRIM YOUR CAT'S NAILS PROPERLY

The best way to trim your cat's nails is really to start handling its paws when it is a kitten. Gently grasp the paw and massage them until the claw pops out. Work on each separate claw and should your kitten get tired of this, let it go and don't make a big deal about it. Do it gently and your little kitten will soon get used to it, especially if you combine it with petting that the kitten has shown a liking for, such as stroking him or her under the chin.

You can usually teach an older cat to tolerate their claws being played with in the same way, though it may take longer. Adding a little treat if they sit still long enough to do all the claws on one paw is enough usually for one time. So don't push it otherwise the cat will know something is going to happen and disappear quickly as they are quick to pick up anything odd or strange that is being done or is going to be done to them.

Sit the cat on your lap and turn its face outwards while you play with the paws. Do not exert too much pressure, as the part that the claws is sheathed in is like the finger where the nails is, not covered in much skin at all, and hurts very quickly if you push hard on it. A cat extends its claws very quickly, so it is usually very easy to get them extended if you practice for a bit, without making a big deal about it again.

At no time allow your children to cut the cat's claws, for they may not see where the quick is and give a nasty painful cut to the claw, ensuring the cat never allows you to go near the claws again. If you can't do it yourself or with the help of another grown up person, then take the cat to a salon that specializes in this type of work, or even to the vet. It is worth the money for the cat will never fully trust you again if you simply scruff it and attack, and you may find your cat even runs away from home, never to be seen again for some reason.

Claws that need trimming are usually long, like fingernails or toenails and may be split or frayed. On dark colored claws, it can be hard to see the quick, where the nail is darker, so simply tip them and cut away the frayed parts, but do not trim the sides of the nail. A very sharp pair of nail scissors can be used, but special scissors can be bought to do this grooming job also.

SOME FUN WAYS TO
ENTERTAIN YOUR CAT

Cats can amuse themselves quite well without human interference, but sometimes we like to have more interaction with our cat or cats. We just might like our curtains left hanging up and not on the floor with a very upset cat tangled in them. Climbing around on top of a cupboard is also highly entertaining to a cat, as is knocking everything down while it tries to catch a bug or a fly, which was foolish enough to show itself.

If you prefer your cat to use far less energy but still get exercise then use the light of a laser pen to amuse him or her. Moving the light from the laser pen along a wall can give your cat quite a bit of exercise as it tries to catch the light, and the look of absolute concentration they can achieve while catching the beam you will rarely see on any other animal.

An empty toilet roll gives kittens especially good exercise if you can roll it until the cat or kitten grabs and rolls around with it. Cats though, are very insecure about their dignity and it is no surprise to find, if you burst out laughing for too long, to see the cat stalk off with its tail in the air and an expression of ' You are here to entertain me, I am not here to be laughed at' on its face. Kittens are not as easily insulted as will be seen in most games you can play with them.

A ball of wool can involve much catching, throwing and kicking with the back feet. Don't use a ball of wool that you are going to be using later for some knitting though as you will find it very frayed after a few games of this. Proper wool does not take too kindly to this treatment, but the synthetic will to a certain extent. Try not to let the cat or kitten chew off bits of the wool and swallow it either, because it may turn into a hairball.

If your house has a reasonably long hallway in it, then a ping pong ball can provide fun for a while. Some cats will even learn to retrieve the ball, but be prepared for teeth marks, as the difference between a dog's mouth and a cat's is quite large. A dog can grip a ball without damage, but a cat must hold the ball between its teeth properly in order to carry it, much the same, as it would prey. A ping pong ball is too large to fit in-between a cat's teeth like a dog's, so they must bite it hard in order to carry it. Simply roll the ball along the hallway and allow it to bounce off the walls until your kitten or cat grabs it.

HOW TO CLEAN YOUR CATS EARS CORRECTLY

Cat lovers out there are always worried about cleaning their cat's ears without hurting them and in the right way. Regular care is essential for keeping your cat's ears from mite infestations and other such infections. A routine inspection and cleaning can detect any such infections well in advance and can take necessary steps to avoid severe health problems.

Cats' ears normally gets problems such as allergies, bacterial or yeast infections, mite infestations and fungal infections. When practiced on a regular basis, cleaning and inspecting your cat's ears from a very small age, as most cats normally gets used to it without having any issues. The following aspects need to be kept in mind while caring for your cat's ears.

Make the cat feel comfortable when you clean the ears. You can treat your cat to some snacks while you carry on with the ear cleaning. Make sure that the cat is in a happy mood. This means that, you should never try to clean an angry cat's ears or just after a bath, etc...

Handle with good care and make sure that you are holding the cat in a position that is much comfortable for the cat so that the cat doesn't get hurt from being excited.

You can use your forefinger and thumb to roll up the inner skin of your cat's ears, whereby you can clearly see the inner surface of the ears to clean the area. You can also use your remaining fingers to get a good grip on your cat, in order to hold him or her without sliding from you.

Look for any waxy substances and discharges inside the ears. Light brown color wax is normally seen in all kind of cats, which is a good indication as the cat is having natural ear care. But, if the discharge is of dark brown, black, green or yellow in color, it needs attention as it indicates some sort of infection. Pus and such discharges can be wiped away gently with an ear cleaning pad before taking further steps.

You can also drop some five to ten drops of an ear cleansing liquid into your cat's ears and massage the outer base portion of his or her ears for few seconds. A cotton ball can be used to clean the inner surface after the above cleansing is done.

If you see your cat is shaking his or her head more than usual or if he or she seems to scratch their ears frequently, then it might need a veterinarian's attention and further medical care. Make it a routine to inspect your cat's ears along with a regular body checkup. In this way you can assure your pet a healthy and fit life.

WHAT YOU SHOULD KNOW ABOUT CAT TEETH

Oral care is one of the most significant parts when it comes to the overall healthcare of your beloved cat. Cats especially are a group of pets that requires extreme personal attention. The cat's mouth in the wild is a lot more different from the ones that are domestic. The former gets its oral care done naturally when it chews on different materials while it catches its preys in the wild etc... Whereas the latter is mostly fed with packed food which even though is much rich in terms of a healthy diet, adds on to poor oral care. Hence much care needs to be given manually to your lovely domestic cat.

It is always better that the pet owner himself or herself doing a routine oral examination of the pet at home. You can do this by putting one hand at the back of the cat's head, whereby gently stroking the cat you can take a look at the front teeth of the cat by lifting the upper lips with your fingers. You can do this examination at one side first. This will aid in examining the gums and the other part of the teeth.

If you think that the cat will cooperate, you can try prying the mouth open by slowly pushing its lower jaw down gently. Now, even if your cat doesn't allow you to get a detailed examination, a quick observation while he or she yawns will give you an idea on any overall discoloration or so. Nothing is equal to brushing the cat's teeth on a daily basis, when it comes to cat's oral care.

One important thing to keep in mind while caring for your cat's teeth is that, never try to use human friendly things for a cat, unless it is proven non harmful. Some people tend to use human tooth paste for example for cleaning their cat's teeth, which is in fact never a good idea. There are cat friendly tooth pastes available which are mainly flavored with malt, meat and fish for cat's likeability. The best part of such tooth paste is that they are specially made for cats and hence rinsing is not required and the purpose is met by swallowing the paste. Also, available in the market are cat tooth brushes and oral cleaners, you would be surprised!

Even though the above said is an easy way for cleaning your cat's teeth, nothing is as equal as cleaning it manually with a brush. This might appear tedious, but if you practice with your cat this habit from when it is a kitten, then the matter can be solved easily! If you might have acquired your cat when he or she was full grown, it is better to follow the toothpaste swallowing procedure as otherwise it can even end up in harmful situations for both the cat as well as the owner.

Always remember to feed your cat with specially made foods that are designed to clean up their teeth, do regular checkups and give special attention during any unusual symptoms.

HOW TO MAKE SURE YOUR CAT IS EATING A HEALTHY AMOUNT OF FOOD?

Cats are well known as finicky eaters among all other pets out there. The truth is that, yes cats are a bit choosy, whatever breeds it belongs to. They prefer a proper diet rather than a changing menu. They have a great sense of taste and smell. Most cat lovers get confused on checking out whether their cat is taking a healthy and considerable amount of food on a daily basis. This can be answered if you invest some time in studying the cats' eating habits in detail.

Cats are pets that love to follow a systematic eating habit which involves a routine diet, feeding time etc. They prefer not to share their food with some other pets (even if it's a cat!). A sudden change in the menu will not be welcomed at all. They would rather prefer a new food item being gradually introduced along with larger portions of their favorite items. You also need to look into the nutritional requirements of the cat's food sold out there in the market. This is because cats are one set of animals that requires some unusual nutrition. This includes Vitamin A, taurine, niacin and essential fatty acids.

The amount of food and frequency of feeding is of great concern. Kittens, usually less than twelve weeks of age needs to be fed at least 4 times a day. An adult cat can be fed twice a day. You also need to keep in mind things such as, never allow your cat to roam around in a neighboring house, developing a begging behavior by feeding with scrap food etc., all of which can lead the cat to have a bad habit routine.

As with cats, it has been seen that they prefer to consume well and stay healthy when you feed them with meat based cat's food rather than a vegetable based one. Canned and moist food is also preferred by cats. But you need to make sure that you're moist and canned foods are never left behind if not eaten. Once opened, the dry foods can be used as a tooth cleaner while kept in a feeding pan for the best part of the day, which also serves as a snack for the cats.

Plenty of clean water is also a necessity with cats as with any other animals. But make sure that you provide them with clean and non-contaminated water as they are choosy even when it comes to water. If your cat gets around to eating some leaves and grasses, it might be a possible indication of improper diet.

Always make sure that you feed your cat on time with a regular routine. Never hesitate to get a veterinarian's consultation when you suspect any sort of abnormalities with the cat's eating habits. Remember, a healthy cat is the one that follows his or her personal cat's routine.

THE DIFFERENT KINDS OF WORMS CATS CAN GET

Worms are always a trouble to cat owners, when it comes to taking care of their health. To aid the treatment, it is a necessity to identify the type of worms that your cat has got. Here are some worms that cats usually get. There are mainly three types of worms that cats can normally get. They are: Tapeworms, Roundworms and Hookworms.

Out of the 3 types of worms, the most common culprit is tapeworms.

Tapeworms: Cats usually get tapeworms from eating meat that is uncooked, rodents or even from fleas that are infected. These worms get into the walls of cat's intestine and passes out its eggs along with the cat's stool. Worm segments or eggs can be identified from the cat's stool, which usually will be pinkish or whitish in color. In severe conditions, worms are also seen in cat vomit. Other symptoms include weight loss, reduced appetite, bony appearance, hair loss etc. Treatment is available where tablets for deworming are normally prescribed.

Roundworms: Ascarids are the most common type of round worms. These cylindrical worms are pointed at both ends with white body color. They are mostly infected via preys such as cockroaches or rodents. Kittens get ascarids mainly through mother's milk. Symptoms are almost similar as that of tapeworms. Kittens are normally seen to possess higher levels of threats in cases of roundworm infestations. As the ascarid worms are slightly resistant when compared with tape worms, a regular cleaning of stools and litter pans is advised.

Hookworms: Hookworms are less common in cats, and are found in hot and humid areas. Rotten meat preys and breast feeding are potential entry points for hook worms. Penetration through the skin is possible for larvae which later migrate to the small intestine of the cat. Severe diarrhea, anemia, stools which are dark red or black in color, rashes in between the toes etc., are common symptoms.

Usually a hookworm infestation of severe cases needs your cat to be admitted with the veterinarian for complete cure. Also the litter pans and stools need to be cleaned off from time to time with hot water.

If you suspect your cat to be infested with any kind of worms, remember to take a sample of its stool to your vet and get a test done as a preliminary step. Also, follow the vet's advice in getting your dewormer, as some dewormers can be toxic with higher dosages. If you decide to continue on buying such dewormers from a pharmacy, it might not also work on all worms.

You need to be careful with cross contamination issue as well, whereby in a multi cat atmosphere (household) necessary arrangements need to be done to separate and identify separately each cat's stools. Their pans and belongings should also never be interchanged with other cats

HOW TO DEWORM YOUR CAT

Owning a pet, especially a cat can be a lot more stressful, if not enough attention and care is given to the animal's health issues. Vaccinations and other treatments are needed from time to time for cats. Along with all such care, deworming them is equally important as well.

Cats, especially the kittens and the old ones are much more prone to worm infestation. Kittens are mostly born with some kind of worm infection, through their mother's milk. Old cats are also easier in getting infected through their surroundings. Knowing in detail the type of worms and the deworming methods will aid in approaching a vet for help.

Deworming should be of your prior concerns when it comes to stray cats. Cats that come with a greater linking for preys are of 100% sure, carriers if worms. There are mainly 3 types of worms that infect cats, tapeworms, roundworms and hookworms. Tapeworms get into the walls of cat's intestine and passes out its eggs along with the cat's stool. Roundworms are mostly infected via preys such as cockroaches or rodents. Kittens get ascarids mainly through mother's milk. Rotten meat preys and breast feeding are potential entry points for hook worms.

A sample verification of the cat's excreta at the vet is the first step in identifying the infection and furthering the treatment methods. These worms can have longer inactive periods and quick active stages which might make the identification tedious at times.

Most deworming medications either come as pills or in liquid form. You need to remember that most cats are choosy and have a keen sense of taste and smell and might not properly consume the medicine for deworming. It is advised to follow the disguising technique whereby deworming medications are mixed along with the cat's food while feeding them.

This can be the hardest part for most cat owners when deworming is required. Never give the cats the pills straight away, as chances of them spitting or vomiting it out is pretty good. Deworming needs to be considered as a combined treatment method where, along with oils or liquids, you might also need to conduct other medications due to the insusceptibility of various growth stages of the worm larvae to the medications.

Prevention is better than cure. Hence make sure that your cats get a proper healthy diet and living conditions for a long and healthy life. If you suspect your cat to be infested with any kind of worms, remember to take a sample of its stool to your vet and get a test done as a preliminary step. Also, follow the vet's advice in getting your dewormer and how to use it properly.

WHAT TO EXPECT WHEN YOUR CAT IS PREGNANT

If you are a cat lover and love to see your cat breeding and extending the family, you need to be well aware of the pregnancy period of the cat and what happens during this time period. Even though cat pregnancy is considerably easily recognizable and taken care as compared with many other pets, it needs utmost care and attention during the gestation period and after birth. Cat's being very close to humans; love to get attention, pampering and care during this particular time period of gestation.

As with many other mammals, it is difficult to say whether a cat is pregnant or not during the 1st week of gestation. This is because, she won't be showing much visible symptoms of pregnancy and behavior also will remain the same. In the next few weeks, if you suspect your cat to be pregnant, the first and foremost thing that you need to do is to check her nipples.

You can do this during the normal regular oral checkup, cleaning time or during the health checkup time. After about 3 weeks of gestation, cats will have their nipples turned pink in color. This is a good indication that the cat is pregnant. Mostly this is clearly visible when she is getting pregnant for the 1st time in her life.

After this period it will take almost another 6 weeks our more to deliver her sweet little kittens... i.e. a gestation period of almost 2 month (8weeks). Even though you can clearly identify the pregnancy from such simple symptoms, it is always better to get it confirmed by your vet.

Once they are under the pregnancy period, they become quieter and love to sleep more than usual. Their heat cycles will be suspended for the time being and their interest in male cats will be lost. The domestic cats that used to love walking and roaming outside will tend to spend much of its time back inside home, mostly sleeping as mentioned just a second ago.

Gaining weight is normal during the pregnancy period and visible weight gain is seen usually till the fifth week of gestation. After the 5th week, the nipples will also grow to a considerable size and will be ready to lactate once the kittens are out. As with their appetite, they will love to eat more during this period and it is pretty good for the mother's health too. You need to feed her with more food, but don't over feed her. Mixing her food with kitten food is good before delivery days. It is also seen that the expecting mother cat drops their appetite at about the 5th week of gestation.

Knowing the cat pregnancy in detail will enable you in taking care of the mother cat and the babies safely, sound and smooth during and after the period of gestation and delivery.

TRICKS YOU CAN TEACH YOUR CAT

One doesn't really think much about tricks you can teach a cat. We are prone to think of the family dog as being the one who will do tricks. It is true that dogs tend to be more eager to please. But there are tricks you can teach your cat that are fun to do and fun to show off to friends when they come to visit as well.

Cats are aloof and they have their own opinions about how things should go. But they still respond to rewards and punishments and to affection and praise. Cats are also quite smart and they will learn that certain behaviors get them food or love. Knowing that cats respond to that kind of stimulation gives you all you need to develop a nice collection of tricks you can teach your cat.

One of the easiest ways to develop a nice routine of tricks you can teach your cat is to offer him or her a treat they love so that he or she gets interested in it every single time. It could be a special commercial cat snack or something as simple as a tiny bit of hot dog or cheese. For example, if you show the treat to your cat and then hide it, he/she will begin to reach out to you to stop you from pulling it away. Repeat this game until he/she "waves" at you and then give her the reward.

Repetition is the key to training any animal so if you repeat this little game, your cat will enjoy playing with you and learn that lifting her paw a certain way will always result in a treat. Before long, all you have to do is lift your fingers like you did when you had the treat and she will "wave" at you on command.

You can use this same technique for lots of tricks you can teach your cat. Repeat the process but instead of teaching her wave, gently touch her paw and "shake" it. Be sure you do not pinch her paw as that will not be accepted as a loving gesture. But that simple shake will become associated with the treat and before long; you can and will know how to shake hands.

The trick that we teach dogs to roll over is easy to add to your roster or tricks you can teach your cat. It is not hard to find a time when your cat rolls over naturally. Cats love to be on their backs and he/she will often do that when you come near in hopes of getting her tummy rubbed. So reward her with that loving rub but before you do so, wave your hand over him or her as a signal that the love is coming to them. If you repeat that motion, they will eventually associate that wave with the tummy rub and roll over for that motion every time.

Using love, play and food, there are many kinds of tricks you can teach a cat. Simply take motions or behaviors that your pet already does naturally and develop them into a trick that he/she will repeat based on a command or a motion and they will perform for you reliably time and time again.

WHY CATS LIKE TO CLIMB UP STUFF

Cats are amazingly athletic in their ability to run, jump and climb. When you think about how powerful their legs are as you watch a cat jump many feet into the air, it makes you glad they are so small and that they like you. Any time you bring a new kitten into the home, you will notice how much they love to climb. It can be pretty aggravating watching a kitten climb up the curtains until you get a chance to train the cat not to do that.

It doesn't have to be a big mystery why cats like to climb up things. You may have the temptation to think that they are doing it to be naughty. But keep in mind that even a smart domestic cat is still an animal and that she does not know that climbing is against the rules until she is trained to stop. That is why knowing why cats like to climb up things will make you more patient with your animal.

When your kitten climbs the curtains or the side of the couch, it is usually in the course of play. It is good to recognize, however that to a cat, play is a rehearsal for real events that happen in the life of an animal in the wild. Even though your cute kitten is a house cat, she has all the instincts that came to her from that history of the species as wild animals. That history included hunting and running away.

Cats who live in the wild must hunt to survive. While your cat does not have that problem, that instinct continues in her just the same. Climbing is a skill that nature gives to the feline species to be able to hunt prey for food. All you have to do is watch your cat chase a squirrel or bird in the back yard to see that instinct in full use. This does not mean that when she climbs your curtains or your leg that your cat is hunting for food. That use of climbing in play is part of how cats are wired as well and it is why cats like to climb up things.

Maybe an even more important skill that any wild animal needs to survive is the ability to escape when being hunted by a foe. All you have to do is play chase with your cat so see how good she is at escaping. The skills that nature gives to even house cats to get away include running, leaping, fighting and climbing. A cat can go up a tree in lightning speed when it is on the run from harm. The problem is that sometimes they cannot get back down.

Understanding that why cats like to climb up things has to do with instinct makes it easier to deal with it when your domestic pet does that. She really is not trying to be bad. It is part of being a cat just as much as purring and cuddling up on your lap.

The good news is that with some gentle training, you can teach a cat to keep those climbing skills for outside and to leave your expensive curtains and furniture alone.

HOW TO MAKE HOME-MADE CAT FOOD

There are a number of good reasons to learn how to make homemade cat food. If you are thinking about going that route, be alert that your veterinarian may discourage it. Keep in mind that most veterinarians sell cat food so they are not interested in seeing the profits of the big pet food companies go down. So take that advice with a grain of salt.

Cost and the health of your cat may be two of the best reasons for learning how to make homemade cat food. It might seem that the fuss and difficulty of creating delicious and healthy food for your cat would be a drawback. But when you think about how much money you are saving not buying "gourmet" cat food for your pet and that fresh food is so much better for your fluffy friend that the fuss and effort will turn into a labor of love that will actually become a fun cooking project for you each week.

It is good to go into the process of learning how to make homemade cat food with the spirit of adventure. You may need to experiment to come up with the perfect recipes to use to make food for your cat. It pays if you have a good feel for what she already likes to eat. Some cats like fish and others like meat, cheese and various vegetables you may mix into your home made cat food.

After you have a good idea what your cat likes, be sure you educate yourself in how to prepare meals that fulfill all of your pet's nutritional needs. There is plenty online to help you make sure you are giving your cat good food and plenty of it. You will have a decision to make when sorting out how to make homemade cat food about whether to cook it or to serve the food to your cat raw. As a rule, it is probably smart to cook meat to avoid any chance of salmonella poisoning.

Cooking the meal also makes it easier to turn into edible cat food in your food processor. This is an important step because when you run the food processor with all of the ingredients in your recipe for how to make homemade cat food, you can be sure nutritious things go in that will not be noticed by your animal because of the good things that are in there that she loves.

You can get more information from your pet store or your veterinarian about any supplements to slip into the mixture when you are running your home made cat food through the food processor. It's a good idea to keep a journal of what you cook for your cat so that you can try different recipes to see how she responds. When you have completed your first batch of cat food for your animal, serve it to her in small amounts so that there is not much left in the dish to go bad.

Once you know how to make homemade cat food, you can store each batch in the refrigerator for a few days. That way, you can make up larger amounts and feed it to her over time. But be careful that you keep your home made cat food fresh and delicious so that your cat loves meal time even more with your recipes than she ever did when she ate that store bought cat food out of the can.

HOMEMADE CAT TOYS YOU CAN MAKE YOURSELF

You never really have to buy a cat toy for your cat when there are plenty of homemade cat toys you can make yourself. Cats make terrific pets but the one thing that any cat owner will tell you is that their cat has a mind of her own.

Part of the charm of a pet cat is that the animal will have her own ideas about what she wants and that idea is not open to negotiation. So when you start to think about getting a fun cat toy for your pet, it is good to think about how she likes to play. As you watch, it is natural to ask if your pet would like a cat toy that you might buy or if you could get by with homemade cat toys you can make yourself.

It is great fun to watch a cat play. Cats are amazingly playful creatures and they will play with you or with just about any object they come across if the cat is in the mood. In fact, many cats can play with things or creatures that do not seem to be there at all. If anyone ever suggested that a cat does not have an imagination, you know better if you have ever seen your cat play with tremendous energy with something that to human eyes is not there.

If you go to a pet store or even to the pet department of your local Wal-Mart or grocery store, you will find plenty of cat toys you can buy. There is nothing more frustrating than putting a new cat toy you paid for in front of your cat only to see her turn away from it in a huff to go play with a bug.

Realistically, you never have to buy a cat a toy. The number of simple items that you already have around the house can be used with great success to keep your cat entertained for hours. Here is a list of simple homemade cat toys you can make yourself.

A string with a ribbon tied to the end will keep a cat amused for hours.

To encourage your cat to have fun hunting, put a feather under a newspaper with the tip out for her to see. She will stalk it all afternoon.

And empty paper bag will become a fort for your cat. Cats love the rustling sound it makes when they run in and out of it.

Things that move are great fun for cats including an ice cube or a small rubber ball. When she swats it and it escapes, she will think it is alive!

Put a little catnip in a sock you don't need and roll it up and put it in another sock. Watch as your pet pounces on that toy over and over again.

The ideas for homemade cat toys that you can make yourself are endless. There is no reason to buy cat toys when your pet will play with all kinds of inexpensive items you have lying around. And if she can play with you as well as with that toy, so much the better for both of you!

WHEN SHOULD YOU SPAY OR NEUTER YOUR CAT?

If you want to know when you should spray or neuter your cat, please read on and learn more. When the ovarian hysterectomy of the female species is described, it is called spraying. On the other hand castrating a male species is known as neutering. Both are surgical treatments and can be done by a qualified veterinarian. This makes the cat incapable of having babies in future. The procedure is very beneficial for you and your cat.

When is the right time to spray or neuter? When the cat is as early as 8 weeks old, the procedure can be done easily, by a qualified vet. It is strongly recommended that they get the neutering done early, since it would be healthier for your cat, and the cat population doesn't increase.

Is it important to have your cat neutered? Yes it is important to have your cat neutered. Take a look at the animal shelters around; there numbers are increasing and the population of cats with them increasing by the day. Would you rather have the current cats neutered and avoid over population or would you want them to grow only to be left out and euthanized later on? Not everyone is a willing adopter, due to many reasons. Some even abandon their pets, again for various reasons, hence neutering your pet helps.

The health and behavioral benefits: When you neuter the cat, he would live a happy life and a longer life, not to forget a healthier life. When you spay the cat, she would be devoid of the mating heat crying syndrome, when she is in heat. Plus there is a lot of mess when the cat is in heat, and she would thank you dearly for getting her spayed on time, which avoids such a mess.

When you neuter the male, he wouldn't have sexual desires, there wouldn't be aggressiveness in him, nor would he want to roam wild and aimlessly.

When you neuter the males, it would prevent cancer of the testicles and his prostate gland wouldn't enlarge, so the risk of having perennial tumors can be ruled out.

Hopefully now you might understand why neutering and spaying the cat would be good for them. Always speak to your vet and then make a decision on whether the pet needs to be neutered or not.

WHAT YOU SHOULD KNOW ABOUT
FLEAS & TICKS

Fleas, Ticks, Mites and Lice are some outer parasites that will drive your cat and you both crazy. It will involve your kitten or cat constantly scratching and biting trying to get the fleas and other parasites off of them. When you see your kitten or cat using their hind legs to scratch their ears, and using their teeth to try and dig into their skin, it's a pretty good sign they have fleas or a more serious problem.

You can usually get rid of most parasites like fleas and ticks with good quality shampoos and more. One of the things you need to remember is that the eggs that these little parasites leave behind, can take from days to weeks to months to hatch. You need to make sure you kill all the eggs on bedding materials and other places your pet frequents and stays.

Fleas are a common problem for kittens and cats, and they are known to carry and transfer tapeworms sometimes. A good flea spray or shampoo, or other products should work fine. They do have other brands that you usually apply once a month, that usually will take care of the problem the best, and are on the more expensive side, but well worth it.

You should not use any chemicals on pregnant or nursing mothers, as this could harm the puppies or new born litter.

Ticks are a problem as they can carry Lyme disease and other diseases. Cats usually get these from trees and bushes, as the parasites fall onto the cat's hair, they then attach themselves to the skin, and suck the blood, and sometimes will suck the blood of humans as well.

If you see a tick on your cat and you want to remove it, do not just pull on it. The head might snap off and stay imbedded into your cat's skin. Use pet shop oil for removing ticks, and try and drown and suffocate the tick, and then use tweezers to wiggle the tick back and forth until the whole body becomes free.

If your cat gets lice, you will be able to spot them pretty easily. You would usually need to get a good quality shampoo or insecticide for lice from your local pet store, and it will usually take several applications to make sure they are gone.

If your cat has mites, it is best to take them to the veterinarian for a checkup, and get special medications for your type of mites. There are many different kinds of mites, so your vet should be able to identify them. Left untreated, it will get worse and worse. Some of the mites to look for are around the ears, with dark spots that look like small scabs, but are actually mites eating your dog. Some mites you cannot see unless the vet uses a microscope, and for this reason, you should take your cat in right away if you suspect mites, and to help get rid of your cats discomfort.

WHAT THE BENEFITS OF MICRO CHIPPING YOUR CAT ARE TO YOU

If you've been wondering if micro chipping your cat is a good thing, it is, if you ask me. It's just like anything, if you ask 7 different veterinarian's the same question, you might get some totally different answers and opinions, so just use your common sense.

A microchip that is placed inside your cat, usually between the shoulder blades, and with a syringe that looks pretty much like the one cats get their shots with. The microchip is about the size of a grain of rice. It is inserted by your veterinarian, and different vets sell different packages, but relatively all the same.

It is really no more painful to your cat then them getting vaccinated. If you ever lose your cat, this is one of the best ways of hoping to get him or her back.

The microchip is basically a transmitter, that the skin just grows right back over, and it stays with your cat, for their entire life. The transmitter does not require any batteries or maintenance. It is embedded with a number the company supplies and your veterinarian will have much more details on, you will have to pay a onetime fee for this service.

When a scanner that a vet or animal shelter should have on hand these days, maybe some smaller out in the country vets still don't have access to one, but if they do, the scanner would make the transmitter give off a signal, that the scanner could read. Since it is universal, injecting the microchip behind the shoulder blades, but over time and years, some cats may have growth movement.

Millions of cats get lost every year. One of the best ways to make sure your kitten or cat does not get lost in the first place, is to be a responsible pet owner. Make sure your home and yard is kitten and cat proof, just like you might do for a real baby in your home.

Make sure fences and gates are secure, make sure there are no holes being dug you don't know about. Make sure your cat gets plenty of exercise and care and love, so they don't feel the need to go elsewhere.

If for some reason your cat becomes lost, the collar and tags might get lost or removed, and then it is nearly impossible to find the rightful owner sometimes, and the worst you can imagine might happen. With the microchip, it is not a for sure bet, but your odds are much higher of getting your lost cat back, then if you did not have it.

Hopefully your kitten or cat has a very nice place to live, either indoors or outdoors, and they like their surroundings, and never dream of running or getting away. But if for some reason, they are in heat, or they hear kids playing, or the mail delivery person coming, and they want to escape, or they just get loose by accident. Like a small child leaving the door open, and then they are long gone, that microchip is going to play a much bigger role in finding him or her, and I really hope it works for everyone!

HOW INVISIBLE FENCING TYPICALLY WORKS TO TRAIN AND PROTECT YOUR CAT

Hopefully this will give you a basic understanding on how invisible fencing for your cat should work, and if it is for you, or not for you. Only you can decide if you agree with invisible fencing. Not all yards are the same, and by no means, not all cats are the same, but it should work for most people that use it correctly.

The system would usually entail you trenching a trench, or digging up the ground along the path you want your invisible fencing to go. Just pretend it is an invisible wall, and where you put the wires, will be where the invisible fencing will be located at.

You would want to check with your local utilities or power company before digging up and installing the wires. But it is not that difficult for the average person, as long as they follow the instructions carefully for the system they purchase.

Your cat would be fitted with a collar that has some sensors that stick out and contact the cat's skin. From what I hear, the cat does not get a shock, but a surprising jolt, and since cats cannot talk, we will really never know what they feel, until we find a cat that can talk. We can put him or her on television, and they can maybe tell us everything that is wrong with cats and kids would love that story, but you get the idea!

The way it works is you bury the wires underneath the lawn, so you don't have wire everywhere. You can also run it along wooden fences, but not metal ones, and that could be a boundary wall, so they don't dig out, but you don't have to dig up that section, because a fence is already there, basically making them stop digging out, or jumping up on the fence any more.

The collar would require batteries, and a test period, and training sessions with your cat, so that he or she understands what is desired of them. You have to train them properly about where they can, and where they cannot go in the yard. They do have systems for inside the home for cats that jump over gates, and you could find that on the internet for inside places.

You would place red flags along the path of the invisible fencing, for training purposes with your cat. Your cat needs to be able to see the invisible lines first. That is what the flags are put in the ground for. A system that is working fine would give the cat several beeps warning him or her that they are getting too close to the fence.

If they do not move back, they will get a shock or surprise jolt, depending on how you look at it, since the cat can't tell us. The part you really need to teach your cat before you let him or her loose or on their own, is to turn away from the fence, and go back.

You could teach them this by turning it into a fun game for both of you. You would train your cat by taking them up to the fence, and when the warning beeping starts to go off, you could turn around and run, and call your cat to come too! Then when he or she comes, you could give them some praise, and teach them to turn back, not go thru it.

Like anything, you would actually need to teach them to go thru it, so they know what they are in for. Walk with them, and when the warning beeping is going off, let them experience the effect of the surprise.

I'm hoping they are getting a surprise rather than a shock, but if this saves them from running out in the street and getting hit and killed by a car or truck. Or getting lose and lost, then I believe they need to learn what happens if they don't come back, while you are there, rather than while you are away.

You would leave the red flags up until you think your cat is ready for them to be taken down. As with anything you love, take good care of your cat, and watch them and keep an eye on them. If you just use common sense, and follow the directions on the kit you buy, and don't take any short cuts, do it right the first time, and it will work. Just plan everything ahead of time, and give your cat plenty of time to learn the new system with you, and you both should be happier and safer!

WHY DO CATS LOVE CATNIP SO MUCH?

No your kitty isn't on drugs or an addict to stimulants if she is on Catnip. In fact Catnip also known by the name catnip or even catmint is known to be safe. It is a perennial herb that occurs on a yearly basis and is a member of the family of mints. Any species of the family of cats would love Catnip, be it lynx tigers, mountain lions, lions, tigers or even your kitty at home.

Cats just love to roll over the herb, rub their face in it and sometimes extend their claws or twist their bodies over a bunch of Catnip as well so if you watch kitty at home doing the same, don't panic and rush to the vet, this is normal, for she loves Catnip.

The reason why kitty behaves that way is because of the strong odor which is emanated from Catnip There is certain oil in the herb which has transneptalactone, a chemical in the herb. The odor of the chemical reminds kitty of a substance which is found prevalent in any cat's urine. And hence kitty behaves strange when a bunch of Catnip is offered to her.

Cats go berserk and behave as if they have been drugged when they consume Catnip, but they are actually far away from being intoxicated or drugged. As mentioned, the herb is very safe for kitty and since it belongs to the family of mints, there isn't anything for you to worry about. It is actually the chemical within the herb which makes the cat behave the way she does when brought in contact with Catnip.

But your home cat may behave very differently to Catnip from what your neighbor's cat may do. Some cats just don't bother all that much about Catnip, they walk away from it as if it is not their thing, while others go bonkers over it. Those that go gaga over Catnip actually are the ones who find the chemical in the Catnip herb in likely presence to the chemical found in another cat's urine. This chemical actually stimulates the organ of the cat which makes kitty feel sensations of touch, sight, smells, tastes, sounds etc.

If kitty reacts to Catnip, she would lick or eat it, or else she may just playfully roll and sniff the herb, that's it. Not all cats would respond because the behavior is an inherited feature, just like we humans need to acquire taste for certain foods, the same goes for the feline family as well. If kitty is very young or if Catnip is offered to an old cat, the reaction would be less as compared to those who are young adults, but large cats such as lions would react to Catnip, irrespective of age. Don't bother if kitty doesn't react to Catnip, not all cats do and that's normal.

In conclusion we can say Catnip isn't addictive. It is like any other treat for kitty, which can be given once a way. The amusing part about this would be the way she behaves once she has Catnip.

THE CAT GRASS STORY

If you have been noticing kitty at home grazing happily on blades of fresh grass, you would have wondered why she does what she does. And this too especially when you serve her the choicest of delicious meals at home. Yet, when she has the chance, kitty would go and chew the grass around like its dessert. However, there isn't anything for you to fret about for her instincts of having a salad or when she pukes it all out.

Actually the grass juice has folic acid which is very important for the cat's healthy lifestyle. This is a vitamin which vets say is available in the mother cat's milk. The vitamin helps the bloodstream of the cat with oxygen production. If there is a deficiency of the vitamin in the kitty, she could suffer in the long run with anemia, even her growth would take a beating because of the lack of the vitamin.

It is still a question of debate on how cats know if they lack folic acid in them or not, even the experts cannot answer that. Folic acid supplements are found in abundant by cats when they roam out of home, which they may or may not get naturally when you serve them their meals at home.

Cats cannot tell you, but vets say that the chewing of grass helps them with bowel movements as well. In fact grass helps as a laxative; it provides fiber and de-worms the cats as well. Even fur and other bulky substances from their intestines are removed with the help of grass. Broad leafed grass helps with bowels and thin leafed grass helps the cat vomit. All said and done, vets still don't give a clean chit to cats chewing on grass as necessary.

They say healthy cats can manage process matter within without any external help, and it is only the sick ones that would chew on grass. Then there are vets who believe just as humans would pop in an antacid after a meal, the cats chew grass to keep their stomachs settled. And then there is a school of thought which opines cats love the taste and texture of grass so they chew it.

But after a short while of chewing away on grass, the cat pukes it out. This is because their internals aren't designed with enzymes to enable digestion of grass, and not because cats are non-vegetarians. Through the process of regurgitation, cats also cough out the fur balls inside their system, thus it is a healthy practice for them to chew grass and then puke say experts. This wouldn't allow the cat to feel uncomfortable and you shouldn't punish kitty for bringing it out.

You may find it really awkward that kitty chews grass, but honestly she loves it and she is benefiting from it, say experts. She wouldn't ever eat large quantities of it and if she does so on a daily basis, she could be telling you that she needs a vet to check her. If kitty is a cat that isn't outdoors all that frequent, you may want to keep an eye on her grass grazing habits and inform your vet for the same.

WHAT TO DO ABOUT CAT URINE

No matter how much you try house breaking your cat, he would pee where he wants, period. And the consequences God forbid would be for you to bear. Having said that, pee of a cat can be smelly, no wonder one of the popular characters on a comedy sitcom sang SMELLY CAT!!

Cats are very picky about everything they do, including peeing. If they don't have a sparkling (according to their standards) watering hole, they would go find another place to do their business. So no matter how many times you tell the cat "This is your place to pee", consider it being told to the birds and the bees, get the drift.

Now cat pee can smell especially if the cat pee is of a male cat that sprays anywhere he wishes to. They are habitual creatures and no matter how many scolding rituals you may have out him through, he will go search for a spot new and clean to do his business. A spot which doesn't smell of his urine that is! So the only way to go about getting rid of the odor is to instantly clean it with cleaners that get rid of the smell on the spot.

What you could do is blot as much as urine possible with the help of paper towels or an old rag. Then take water (3parts) and vinegar

(1part) and place it on the pee spot, for saturation. Do the same thing once again to completely dry the place and when it is dry use a little baking soda to clean up the place. After this take 3⁄4 of hydrogen peroxide (3%) solution and a teaspoon of detergent and mix it with the baking soda. Rub it on the pee spot and with the help of an old brush work in the baking soda mix. When this spot dries up completely, use a vacuum over it and the odor will be gone.

Sometimes cats pee over clothes kept in the laundry, and this would include your bedding, clothing, rugs etc. All you need to do is use one fourth of apple cider vinegar along with a detergent in the washer.

If the cat pees on walls or the floors, instantly wash the area with a cleaner. Then wipe with water to remove all traces of the residue of cleaners. Repeat the step again, and then use a little bleach. The next step would then be to use a bottle spray and use 10:1 water to bleach mix. The area which needs to be cleaned should be well ventilated and don't forget to use rubber gloves when you clean. Spray the area and wait for a minute and then wipe dry with an old rag, the pee smell is gone.

THE DIFFERENCE BETWEEN CAT SPRAYING AND URINATING

There is always a confusion to know where the cat is urinating or spraying, especially when it's a male cat and he does it not in his litter box but outside. In both cases, the situation isn't too pleasant for you to deal with. However when you know the difference between the two, it could bring down the miseries associated with it.

Most cats when trained from the time they are kittens would use the litter box, however they would still mark and spray places for territorial reasons and that too every day. They would mark by spraying for many reasons, one of which is for them to attract a mate for themselves. The second reason being to mark their territory, while the other reasons is to tell the other cats "back off" from their home.

If a cat is stressed, spraying could happen, and some cats spray just to ensure effective communication is achieved with other feline members of the community. Cat spraying is not only a form of urinating, what they actually give out is a mix of glandular secretions and urine. In this you would find a lot of pheromones, which attracts other animals through their sense of smell.

You should look for signs to know if the cat is spraying or urinating. When a cat is spraying it would stand tall with its tail in the air and its bottom held high. But when it urinates to would crouch and squat, with its bottom held towards the floor. There is also a particular smell for spraying that is different from urination. Experts say the best way to stop the cat from spraying would be to get it neutered. And if you think it is stress that is making the cat do this, find out why the cat is stressed, look for signs.

You should keep an eye on the posture of the cat to know if it is urinating or spraying. Cats can be very territorial and thus would use spraying as their method to communicate the same. This would help them tell other cats about the boundaries and lines they conform to for social standing. Such is the non-verbal communication that it goes without rasps and calls, say experts when cats urinate it helps them release pressure from their bladder, so check the posture as described above and you would know if the cat is spraying or urinating.

The best thing to now do is keep an eye on your cat's behavior and follow what we described for you to know if your cat is spraying or urinating. Once again, if you are confused it would be best to observe your neighbor's cat or speak to a vet who would be able to explain it to you better. Spraying and urinating are natural for cats, especially male cats. Spraying can destroy items around over a period of time, so ensure you learn how to avoid that ahead.

THINGS TO KNOW BEFORE GETTING A CALICO CAT

It is very easy to be dazzled by the beauty of its recently-developed cat that it is sometimes easy to forget about some of the more mundane aspects of Calico cat ownership. But if you wish to be a responsible Calico cat owner, no detail should be too small. In this chapter, we take a look at some of the more practical aspects of owning a Calico cat, including the legality of ownership, the possible need for licenses or permits, and the specific requirements for transporting a Calico cat between states or countries. We also take a look at the costs of keeping a Calico , and an overview of the pros and cons of the breed.

Do You Need a License or a Special Permit?

Like with most domestic cats, the regulations and laws governing ownership of Calico cats varies from state to state, and even from country to country. It is imperative that you check with your local legislative agencies to determine the legality of Calico cat ownership, since it is illegal to own them in some states and countries. And because state laws can change over time, sometimes even faster than we think, it might be a good idea to stay constantly updated to check whether any changes in the laws might add restrictions or affect the legality of your pet ownership.

The first thing you have to check is how Calico cats are classified. In general, Calico s are considered hybrid wild cats, not domestic cats, although in some states, later generations of Calico s are already considered domestic cats (usually F6 and onwards). In certain states that restrict ownership of Calico s, no more than F3, F4 or later generations of Calico cats are allowed, while F1 to F2 or F3 that are considered wild animal hybrids are illegal to own, or may require stricter regulations such as on ownership and accommodation (e.g., must be caged).

Be sure to check not just your state law but also your local county law. Local bylaws of town/city may still ban hybrids even if county and state law allows them. For instance, New York state allows ownership of F6 and later generations of Calico s, but they are not allowed in NYC. Needless to say, this can be a potentially chaotic situation if you find out that your local area prohibits or restricts ownership of Calico cats even if your state law does not. A similar situation exists in Canada, where provinces such as Alberta and Saskatchewan have specific restrictions on hybrid cats

As of this writing, states which prohibit or restrict ownership of hybrid cat ownership include Hawaii, Massachusetts, and Georgia.

Hybrid cats are also prohibited in Australia, due to local concerns for the native wildlife, which are already being threatened by domestic feral cats. In the UK, Serval and F1 Calico cat ownership requires a special license, while later generations of Calico cats are essentially legal and require no special license or permit. So before you even buy a Calico cat, do your due diligence, as even transporting or importing Calico cats may also fall under specific regulations.

CITES, or the Convention on International Trade in Endangered Species of Wild Fauna and Flora, apply here since Calico cats are considered covered by CITES. Transporting Calico cats between or across international borders therefore require a permit. Traveling with your Calico across borders also requires a CITES pet passport. Failure to abide among the 170 member nations of CITES means confiscation of your cat, which will most likely not be returned. Take note that international transport also requires a USDA health certificate and a fish and wildlife inspection of your cat. Rabies vaccines should also be up to date.

Do Calico Cats Get Along with Other Pets?

Provided there was proper socialization experience during the first few weeks of the kitten's life, and provided a continuing atmosphere of positive socialization at home, Calico cats can make great buddies with other pets, such as dogs and other cats. Their playful and affectionate nature make them great buddies with other pets at home.

A proviso should be made, however, when it comes to other smaller animals such as rats, mice, birds, fish, and other similar animals that may naturally be considered the natural prey of cats. If you do keep these types of pets, proper supervision should always be exercised.

How Many Calico Cats Should You Keep?

The decision of whether or not you can keep more than one Calico cat is up to you and your capacity for caring for more than one cat. Remember that this is an expensive breed, and the costs of caring for them and boarding then, not to mention the energy investment in their regular grooming, nutrition and diet, and games and exercise, might also take its toll on some.

On the other hand, because the Calico cat is demanding of attention and energy, some owners do recommend keeping more than one Calico cat. This gives your cat a buddy with whom to play with and socialize, thus continually honing his abilities of interacting with other cats, while giving him another playmate - something that can spare owners who are starved of the time it takes to give the Calico cat the attention that they need.

If you are bringing home a female and a male, and you are not intending to breed, please remember to have your cats neutered or spayed. Also exercise due supervision even if you are bringing home cats of the same gender, or of different age ranges, or even of different breeds. It does not happen often, but sometimes friction can happen even among housemates. Weigh the options, and decide accordingly.

How Much Does it Cost to Keep a Calico Cat?

Calico s are one of the most expensive cat breeds around - and this is mostly because of the comparative rarity of the breed, and the difficulty of the process of breeding them. It isn't easy to breed Calico cats, and most male Calico s are sterile until the fourth generation, sometimes even later. Fertile males fetch a hefty price, and so do fertile females of an earlier generation.

But the cost of keeping a Calico cat is not limited to the initial purchase price. You also have to think about their food, veterinary health checks and vaccines, and the various miscellaneous costs including toys, accessories, and even the wear and tear and damage to house furniture - and the costs can easily skyrocket. In this chapter, we present you with a general guideline of the costs of keeping a Calico cat. Keep in mind that these are all estimates, and can easily be higher or lower depending on your area, and the cost of products and services in your region.

Initial Costs

Expect to shell out more during your first year of Calico cat ownership. Aside from the purchase price, costs of transport, registration, and the costs of licensing or permits, you will also have to invest in the cat's vaccinations, spaying or neutering, veterinary checks, microchipping, and the purchase of the various tools and equipment you will need such as pet beds, food and water bowls, an assortment of cat toys and furniture such as scratching posts and others. Also factor in the costs of any changes you will be making in your home for these cats, such as a secure cat enclosure in your yard.

If you are thinking of adopting a Calico cat, you might be able to find one after paying the adoption fee which can range from $100 to 300. The cost of a purebred kitten bought direct from the buyer, however, can vary between generations and among breeders. Simply put, because the Calico cat is so much in demand among cat owners these days, the price can be pretty steep, ranging anywhere from $2,000 to $18,000 and yes, sometimes even higher.

Annual Costs

Don't forget that you will also need to pay for the regular annual expenses such as food, litter and litter boxes, veterinarian fees, grooming fees, and other similar expenses. If you are keeping more than one Calico cat, doubling those expenses is a good estimate, though you might want to add in a little leeway just in case.

Below is a simple table to show you some of the initial and annual costs you will have to budget for if you plan to bring home a Calico cat.

Item	Initial Costs	Annual Costs

Initial Purchase Price	$2,000-18,000 (£1, 540-13,860)	
Pet Equipment and Accessories	$250 (£193.05)	
Microchipping	$20-25 (£15.44-19.31)	
Food		$250-310 (£193.05-239.38)
Cat Litter		$75-150 (£57.92-115.83)
Veterinarian Fees, Spaying or Neutering	$130-170 (£100.39-131.27)	
Vaccinations	$50 (£38.61)	
Worming		$50-75 (£38.61-57.92)
Flea Treatment		$75 (£57.92)
Veterinarian Fees		$50-65 (£38.61-50.19)

Insurance		$95-235 (£73.36-181.47)
Grooming and other miscellaneous expenses		$250-645 (£193.05-498.07)

*Costs may vary depending on location

**U.K. prices based on an estimated exchange of $1 = £0.90

It is a safe bet to say that you will probably have to budget an average of about $1,000 monthly for a single Calico cat. Again, this can actually be cheaper depending on your lifestyle and the prices in your area for services and products, but probably not by too much, as there might always be various unforeseen emergencies cropping up that you will have to factor in. It is highly recommended, in fact, that you set aside a pet emergency fund to draw from whenever those unforeseen emergencies transpire and you need to shell out additional funds for the care of your cat.

What are the Pros and Cons of Calico Cats?

So to sum it all up, here is a brief overview of some of the pros and cons of the Calico cat hybrid breed. Read them carefully, and honestly assess your capacity for caring for one of these cats. If you are leaning more towards the cons, this breed is probably not the right one for you. It takes a unique and dedicated pet owner to provide the right kind of home for one of these unique cats.

Pros for the Calico Cat Breed

- The Calico is a graceful, beautiful cat with a wild look but has been bred down from its wild ancestor, the Serval. They are highly intelligent, with a sense of humor to spare. You'll probably find yourself dealing with a cat that likes pulling pranks around the house - such as dropping things down on you from where it has jumped on the shelf, or head butting you from behind when you didn't even know he was in the room. Life can be fun and full of adventure when sharing a home with one of these cats.

- A Calico cat can be "dog-like" in its temperament in that it bonds closely with its human family, displaying great loyalty and devotion. You'll find one following you around, unwilling to be separated from you. Many Calico s can be taught a few simple tricks such as sit, stay, fetch, lie down, etc. Properly raised and cared for, having a Calico in the house can be a fulfilling and satisfying experience.

Cons for the Calico Cat Breed

- Big cats that require a lot of space - vertical and running around space. They are high energy cats, great climbers, and some are intelligent enough to open drawers and doors. You need a spacious home, with a secure cat enclosure outdoors for one of these cats. They are mainly indoor cats, but they will not thrive in small spaces or apartments.

- Calicos are very active and energetic, and they demand constant attention. They like interactive games and play, and will occasionally pull a prank on their owners. If you don't have the time to devote to them when they are looking for attention (or if they don't have any other cat to play with), all that great energy can turn destructive. If you are out of the house most of the time, or if you spend most of your time on work and don't have time to devote to socializing with and playing with this cat, then this is probably not the breed for you.

- Early generation Calicos, and even some of the later generations, still have their wild ancestry dominant in their personality. Some have been known to hunt, stalk and kill smaller animals in the surrounding areas - which will not work if you live in a busy neighborhood with other pet owners. There have been some Calicos (not all) reported to have become "wild" after reaching the age of sexual maturity. Some experience or knowledge of the behavior of cats in the wild is necessary when such a situation happens, though many experts say that such behavior can be traced back to poor socialization training and processes. Continuous and ongoing socialization and training is, therefore, necessary in caring for a Calico cat.

PURCHASING YOUR CALICO CAT

Compared to some of the more common domestic cat breeds, Calico cats are still pretty rare, and not available worldwide. And because of this cat's sudden rise to popularity, the high demand for such a hybrid cat, and the high cost of purchasing one, it isn't always easy to tell whether you're dealing with a reputable breeder or one who's only in it for the money. And this is a pretty crucial distinction, because it can tell you whether you're going to be getting a healthy Calico kitten who has been properly weaned, bred from healthy and temperamentally suitable parents, and properly socialized before being turned over to its new owner - you. It has been said that the first few weeks of a kitten's life pretty much determines what kind of cat it will be for the rest of its life. So getting a Calico cat from a breeder who knows what he's doing, was able to give the kittens the proper nurturing and care it needed early on, and has knowledge and experience enough to assess whether you are a good fit for a Calico cat of which particular generation, can actually save you a lot of frustration and heartache later on. Despite the high demand and great popularity of this breed, the Calico cat is not for everyone.

In this chapter, we take a look at some of the options you can explore as you search for that Calico kitten just for you.

Where Can You Buy Calico Cats?

Before you start plunking down money for a purebred Calico kitten, you might want to explore the possibility of adopting a rescue. The sad truth of it is that despite the recent development of the Calico breed, the growing number of irresponsible breeders and owners who lack the commitment needed to care for their Calico cats have resulted in a growing number of Calico cats appearing in rescues and shelters. Many were simply surrendered because the owners found that they could no longer deal with the unique behavioral traits of the Calico - things they should have already learned before bringing one home!

If you are willing to put in the time, energy, effort and commitment to care for one of these special cats, and if you have the resources and the capacity (and the space) that would be ideal to make a home for a Calico, then there is simply no reason why you should not explore the possibility of adopting one who was abandoned by its owner simply for being what it is. For one thing, adopting from a shelter is a lot cheaper than purchasing one directly from a breeder. For another thing, there are a growing number of Calico cats ending up in shelters who simply need an owner who gets what

Tips for Selecting a Healthy Calico Kitten

Once you have found the right breeder, the only thing remaining is to wait for your kitten. It is likely that you are going to be asked to pay a deposit or reservation fee. And given the current popularity and high demand for Calico cats, it is also likely that you will find yourself listed at the tag end of a waiting list. If so, just be patient. Getting a cat isn't a matter of simple shopping, after all.

Once the litter is born, and the weeks before they are fully weaned are approaching, you might be wondering how to best select the kitten that is right for you. You will be living with this kitten for the cat's entire lifespan, after all, so it is only reasonable that you think carefully about how to pick your kitten. Besides which, it is always a good idea to make sure that you are getting a healthy and well-adjusted kitten before you even bring them home. Below are a few guidelines you can follow as you make the acquaintance of the kittens for the first time:

- A healthy kitten should have a clean coat, bright, clear eyes, clean and pink ears, and a well-filled out body. Beware of signs of sneezing or sniffling, discharges in the corners of the eyes, or signs of flea dirt at the base of the tail - which can look like small patches of black sand.

- A well-socialized kitten should be naturally curious and playful, not too forward or aggressive, friendly, active, and not averse to being held. That means that there has been enough socialization between the kitten and its siblings to teach him his boundaries, and between the kitten and the breeder to ensure proper socialization with humans.

- Needless to say, the kitten should, by now be fully weaned. He should no longer be nursing from his mother, but is fully capable of eating on his own. And while you may not have occasion to see this for yourself - a kitten should already be competent with the uses of the litter box. You might want to ask the breeder about this, and whether the kitten has any quirks regarding this - such as sharing a litter box with his siblings, or separate boxes for his pee and poop.

- The kitten must have already had its first shots - and the breeder will provide you with the proper records for this, including a schedule of the subsequent vaccinations needed.

Calico -Proofing Your Home

More commonly-referred to as kitten-proofing your home, Calico -proofing is not unlike baby-proofing, or kitten-proofing, in that you have to ensure that your home is safe for your Calico kitten. The only difference is that you have to take into account the Calico 's considerable climbing ability, as well as their characteristic curiosity, playfulness, and high levels of energy.

It's probably a good idea to confine your kitten to a single room in the beginning, at least for the first few days or so. This at least helps you to ensure that they are well-acquainted with the litter box, and for your kitten, helps him to adjust gradually to new surroundings. After all, he has just been separated from his mother, his siblings, and his old home, and thrust into a completely different home with relative strangers. Best to allow him to make the transition a little at a time - or one room at a time, anyway. Provide him with all he needs within this room. Meanwhile, if you haven't already, take a look at the rest of the house and try to see if you can spot any potential danger areas or zones you might want to address.

Here are a few things you might want to watch out for:

- Secure loose wires, loose cords or cables, and curtains or table cloths that reach all the way to the floor. Kittens seem to like playing with dangling things such as wires or threads and the like, but strong curtain cords, electrical cables, or any other loose wires should be off limits to these cats. You don't want them getting strangled accidentally, or worse, electrocuted should they even think of chewing on those wires.

- No breakables or dainty, precious pieces out in the open. And this goes for shelf spaces, too. Your Calico cat will grow up sooner or later, and even as a kitten, it might already develop a propensity for jumping. And because this is a highly energetic breed with a penchant for playing, don't tempt them by leaving out breakable, valuable pieces out in the open.

- Secure dangerous, poisonous things around the home, such as poisonous plants, house cleaners or chemicals, medicines, pesticides.

- Aside from those dainty pieces, you might also want to secure heavy objects that may be liable of falling and possibly hitting your kitten with a thump.

- Store away small items such as small displays, toys, plastic bags, rubber bands, or other objects which he can possibly chew and swallow, and which might eventually lodge in his throat.

- Secure open containers of water, including toilet lids. Calico s have a particular fondness of water, but that does not mean that all types of water are healthy or safe for them. You don't want them drowning in a tub full of water, an outdoor well, or even the toilet bowl - the latter of which cannot be sanitary. Exercise due caution.

- If your kitten has access to an open balcony or terrace, or a stairway, don't assume that he won't try to jump. Kittens don't have an inbuilt sense of safety, and Calico s are, after all, great jumpers. Sure he may eventually grow up able to scale the highest point of your house, but as a kitten, that is not quite likely. You can probably use a wire netting or something similar to ensure he doesn't somehow slip through.

- A Calico kitten will likely be underfoot many times, and will probably have the sense of adventure to explore the nooks and crannies of your home when you aren't looking. Look inside the washer and dryer before you turn it on. Be careful about opening and closing doors, before turning on the vacuum cleaner, lighting the fireplace, opening and closing the refrigerator, and even turning on or leaving a hot stove.

CARING FOR YOUR NEW CALICO CAT

Bringing a Calico kitten home can be the beginning of a new adventure for you and the rest of your household. It can sometimes be frustrating, maybe even exasperiating, but undertaken with the right attitude and the proper understanding of what a Calico cat needs, it can be extremely rewarding.

The first thing you have to understand is that Calico cats are, in some ways, different from most domestic cats. They are more energetic, for one thing, and they are not likely to want to lie around all day and sleep when they could be playing around with you instead. This can lead to what some might consider problem behaviors, but which are, in truth, simply the unique nature of Calico cats that you must take into consideration when you bring one of these glamorous cats home. Making sure you know what is involved in caring for a Calico , and making the appropriate household preparations, will ensure a better understanding between you and your new feline family member.

Habitat and Exercise Requirements for Calico Cats

Calico cats are not lap cats. They will not sit and purr quietly in your lap, even if they can fit comfortably on your lap. These are moderately to large cats, and many don't like being picked up or restrained in any way. They are quite affectionate, sometimes even dog-like in showing their loyalty, following you around the house, butting your legs with their head to signal their desire to play. The breed has excess energy to spare, and while their primary home should be indoors, they should also be allowed regular outdoors time, whether within a fenced enclosure or on a leash.

Some vertical space will be needed by the Calico , as this breed is a great climber. Don't think in terms of how high they can climb, because they will pretty much reach the highest climbable point in your house - whether it is the shelves, the top of drawers and cabinets, or the fence keeping them in. Even if you watch them for a while and determine that "this fence he cannot climb" - consider his wild ancestry, his excess of energy, and his natural curiosity, persistence, and agility - and with enough time nothing is beyond his reach. So prepare your house accordingly. Clear the shelves above and below of precious and breakable things, and provide your Calico cat a safe enclosure with a secure top out in your yard.

Because of its considerable energy levels, some form of daily exercise is required - whether it is in the form of walking (on a leash) or games and play. You will likely want to work in half an hour or so of walking and as much as that, or more, time for games. This breed loves interaction as much as it does physical exertion, especially if it means that he gets to demonstrate his playful, affectionate nature with you, his owner. Provide them with a wide assortment of safe toys (toys that he won't be able to swallow and thus cause an emergency crisis) to keep him occupied. You don't have to spend a lot of money for this - many household items like cardboard boxes, tennis balls, some chew toys, and a bunch of other simple items to mix it up should suffice. Be aware also that this cat has a fondness for water - and they will paw at shallow bowls of water, dip into aquariums, or sometimes even learn to open faucets and showers! Just be sure not to leave large and open containers of water around - especially tanks of water that are larger than your cat, unless you want them to risk the possibility of drowning.

Given their size and their natural activity levels, Calico cats must be allowed sufficient running room inside the house. If you are not able to give them a room of their own - you must provide them ample space that would at least contain their sleeping area and bed, their food and water bowls, their litter box, some vertical space for climbing, and enough room for running around and playing. If you ensure that you afford them these basic things, chances are you'll keep them happy and content in their new home.

Toys and Accessories for Calico Cats

You'll probably want to provide your Calico cat with a wide selection of toys and accessories to begin with. Just remember to steer clear of breakables, toys with removable parts that are small enough to be swallowed, small foam balls, toys with strings or ribbons, or toys with any lead content. You'll probably discover that your cat will develop a certain fondness for one or two of these toys - each cat will prove individual and unique in this case - and after this fondness is spent, he will move on to other, new favorites. Such are cats. Some recommended toys include tennis balls, cardboard boxes, cat wands, crumpled paper, stuffed animals that are also chewable, and other similar toys.

You might also want to provide him with a suitable scratching post not only to spare your rugs and other furniture from his nails, but also to provide him with a handy way of stretching their spine and sharpening their (hopefully, regularly-trimmed) nails. And because these cats are great climbers, providing them with enough climbing perches and boxes to hide in should provide them an enjoyable habitat to play in.

The Calico as an Indoor Cat

Most breeders and experts are in agreement regarding this one thing about Calico cats: this is a breed that should not be allowed to roam freely outdoors. Because of the Calico 's natural curiosity, and their penchant to follow anything that attracts them, they are extremely high risk for meeting vehicular accidents. Not only that, Calico cats are still relatively rare and expensive enough to be considered fair game for anyone with malicious intent looking to make a buck. Don't chance it. Experts say that cats kept mostly indoors have a considerably longer life span than those who are allowed to roam freely outdoors. These indoor cats are usually healthier, too - because they avoid the temptation of eating unhealthy things, being poisoned, being attacked by other animals, and being exposed to diseases or viruses from other cats and stray animals.

MEETING YOUR CALICO CAT'S NUTRITIONAL NEEDS

It can sometimes feel like feeding your cat should be a simple thing, but at the same time is the most complicated thing when you are faced with the wide variety of cat food available in the market. There is a wide range to choose from, and many claim themselves to be the best in the market for your cat. Recently, many people are turning the tables on commercial cat food companies, feeding their cats homemade food, which they claim is healthier. It goes without saying that Calico owners must wonder if their hybrid cats require specialized nutrition or diet different from most domestic cats? This chapter contains an overview of some of the basics of feline nutrition, tips on how to choose high quality cat food brand, and various other tips and guidelines when it comes to feeding your Calico cat.

The Nutritional Needs of Cats

You've probably come across the phrase, "Cats are obligate carnivores." But what does that really mean?

Think of any cat in the wild, and how they survive. What do they eat? Cats are predators, natural hunters, and the bulk of their diet in a natural environment usually consists of raw meat. Even now, many domestic cats hunt and eat mice, while many feral cats that live on the outskirts of human society mainly live on prey: mice, birds, and other small animals. Now think of what packaged cat food contains. The question to ask yourself now is whether they are getting the same nutrients that they need from cat food as they would be getting from their natural diet?

It is a legitimate question. We all know that we are what we eat - and this applies to humans as well as cats. Many instances of diseases and illnesses, in fact, can likely be traced back to poor diet and nutritional habits. We want to keep our cats healthy, so what do we feed them? Some owners have converted to raw meat and homemade diets, but this is not for everyone. For one thing, feeding them a steady diet of raw meat might actually make thing worse. How sure are you that you are not ignoring their other nutritional needs which they get from food other than meat? And for another thing, raw meat is a fertile breeding ground for bacteria, and unless you know what you're doing, you could actually make things worse for your cat. Consult with your veterinarian before undertaking such a drastic dietary change.

In many instances, perhaps all you need to do is to find the right kind or mix of cat food. In order to do this, the first thing you have to learn is what comprises a balanced feline nutritional diet.

Proteins

Cats derive their protein requirements mainly from meats rather than vegetables, as their digestive system might not be particularly suited to digesting too much fiber and grains. Proteins help build tissues, organs, and help in the production of antibodies and a healthy immune system.

Amino Acids

It is important that your cat's diet contain the essential amino acids that he needs because cats cannot synthesize them in quantities sufficient to meet his needs. Of the different amino acids such as methionine, leucine, tryptophan, lysine, valine, arginine, histidine, phenylalanine, and isoleucine, special mention needs to be made of taurine. Most Calico breeders agree that compared to other cat breeds, Calico cats seem to require more Taurine - which helps in fetal development and the prevention of heart and eye disease. Amino acids can mostly be derived from protein sources such as meats.

Fats

Fats are a concentrated energy source, and are also used by the body for the absorption of fat-soluble vitamins. They also help in digestion, provide protection for the internal organs, and gives the cat's body insulation.

Carbohydrates

Some carbohydrates are necessary for your cat as these help maintain the health of the intestines and also supply energy to some critical organs. But please remember that high fiber sources are not good for all cats, especially kittens. Good fiber sources for cats must be moderately fermentable.

Vitamins and Minerals

Many vitamins and minerals that are necessary in a cat's diet should also be supplied in their diet because cats cannot synthesize them in their bodies. These help maintain a cat's metabolism, bone and teeth health, among others. Please remember that it is never a good idea to provide your cat with vitamin and mineral supplements unless specifically prescribed and approved by your veterinarian.

Water

Like most mammals, cats need water to survive. Keeping them properly hydrated by providing them with a ready supply of clean drinking water can actually keep many illnesses at bay.

How to Select a High-Quality Cat Food Brand

The selection of high-quality cat food should not be based on advertisements or commercials, but on what you see on the label of the product itself. It is important, therefore, that you learn to read the label and ingredients list of a packaged cat food, to determine which is better than others. Below are a few tips to guide you as you search your way down that aisle:

- Look for age-appropriate cat food. You won't feed the same food to a kitten as you will to a senior cat, or to an adult cat. These differences have to do with the specific nutritional needs of the cat in these various life stages. Growing cats need different nutrition compared to adult cats or cats that are past their prime. This is also called the nutritional adequacy statement.
- Look at the label. What is the cat food called? Avoid those calling the cat food various labels such as "meal," or "dinner," or "formula" These labels are usually applied for foods that contain

more than 25%, but less than 95% of the main ingredient. Opt for simpler labels, such as "tuna cat food," or "chicken cat food." Apparently, manufacturers can only do this if the product contains at least 95% of the ingredient named, which means you are at least assured that you are getting a meatier product. Avoid qualifiers such as "with," and "and." Prefixing other ingredients with these qualifiers may make you think that you are getting more quality for you money, but the truth is that these add-ons can mean as little as 3%, while it also allows them to decrease the first ingredient to lower than 95%, as long as the two stated ingredients add up to at least 95%.

- Next, look at the ingredients list. Remember when we said that cats are obligate carnivores? This means that the primary ingredient of the cat food must be quality meat such as chicken, lamb, beef, etc. Always look at the first few ingredients, as manufacturers are legally required to list ingredients in descending order based on weight. In short, the product contains more of the ingredients that are listed first. These should primarily be meat-based.

- If you are not sure whether dry or canned cat food is better, you might want to try a mixture of the two. It seems that historically, cats derive most of their water from the food that they eat -

and even until now, they don't really have a reliable sense of thirst. Make sure that they stay properly hydrated by including some water content in the meal itself, which means canned food. On the other hand, dry food keeps better, and can even be left freely in the bowl for the cat to eat whenever he gets hungry. Mixing up your options can provide some variety to your cat, as you may find him getting bored of the usual fare after too long. In fact, it's probably good idea to have a ready list of good cat food brands just in case your cat begins hankering for something new.

- Good sources of carbohydrates include brown rice, barley, oats, and other whole grains. Avoid, as much as possible, corn meal, corn meal gluten, and wheat gluten. These are cheap fillers and may actually be harmful to your cat.

Don't forget that ultimately, the best judge of which cat food is better is your cat. Try to notice if your cat shows any signs of change - whether for the good or for the bad - whenever you change their regular diet. Remember not to make any drastic dietary changes without your veterinarian's approval, and always give your cats time to adjust to new food by gradually in order to give them a chance to adjust.

Dangerous Foods to Avoid

TICA has advised that feeding Calico cats are not unlike how you would feed most cats - and it is really your choice whether you opt for dry, canned, or a raw meat diet for your Calico. Just make sure that this is an informed decision on your part - and that you are undertaking any dietary changes with the full approval of your veterinarian. This is important because your cat's unique health conditions may not warrant such changes as you would like to make, or it may interfere with medications he may currently be on. This also applies to your decision on how to feed your cat - whether free feeding or based on a regular schedule. Many times, it really depends on your unique situation.

Just remember that not all foods are safe - and some human foods can actually be lethal for felines. Below are some human foods that are actually dangerous for cats. Take note of them, and make sure that none are within easy reach of your cat.

- Alcohol
- Candy and Gum
- Chives
- Chocolate
- Coffee
- Dairy Products
- Energy Drinks

- Fat Trimmings and Bones
- Garlic
- Grapes and Raisins
- Mushrooms

TRAINING YOUR CALICO CAT

The Calico cat is not a cat for everyone, especially not for first time cat owners. Even some of the more experienced feline lovers will find that living with a Calico presents them with some unique and interesting challenges. Highly intelligent and with great energy and motivation for play, Calico s need a lot of attention. While extremely loving and loyal, this is a high energy and playful breed whose natural propensity for games and demands for attention can quickly turn destructive if not trained properly early on. If you don't have the time, energy or the patience to socialize and play regularly with your Calico , then this is probably not the cat for you.

That said, being able to interact and bond regularly with your Calico , nurturing his natural instincts while keeping his behavior under control can be a most rewarding and worthwhile experience. In this chapter, we look at some of the basics of training for your Calico , including socialization, litter training, tricks training, and addressing potential problem behaviors.

Socializing Your New Kitten

Proper socialization is a must, and is likely what will ensure the health and survival of the kitten. Like most babies, kittens pretty much absorb what they need to know to survive during the first few weeks of their life - learning from their mother, their littermates, and you. They learn how to cover their pee and poo from their mother, they learn how to restrain their hunger impulses once the mother no longer feeds them whenever they want, they learn how to deal with other cats such as their mother and their siblings - and what it means to restrain themselves from too much biting and scratching in play, and most of all, they learn how to deal with humans and most of strange things they will find in the human world.

Raising a properly socialized kitten means that your cat is less likely to grow up scared and frightened by each new stranger it meets, or each new sight, sound and smell she is exposed to. Can you imagine the stressful life a cat must lead if it tends to jump in fear at every sound? Now imagine how many strange sounds a cat will find in your home alone - TV, radio, furniture moving around, phone ringing, appliances going off, children running around. A well-adjusted cat begins as a properly socialized kitten, which simply means that he was exposed to a number of things early on in his life within a positive situation so that he learns not to perceive everything strange and new as a threat.

They key to socialization is not to rush things. First of all, a kitten should not be taken away from its mother before it is ready. It may be fully weaned, but is it ready for complete separation with everything it has known since then? Some kittens also do experience separation anxiety. Previously, breeders considered the age of separation to be at around 8 weeks, when the kittens were fully weaned. More recently, however, some breeders were prolonging the separation age from 10 to 12 weeks. It isn't just about the readiness to be separated from its source of milk. It's also about how ready a cat is to be separated - which mostly depends on how its first human socialization experience has proceeded until then. It has been said that a cat's crucial time for socialization experience happens within the first 7-8 weeks of its life, though there is still a window that extends up until it reaches 7 months. Ideally, however, those first few weeks has been packed full of caring and nurturing from both you and its mother, lots of interactive play with other kittens, and enough human handling so that it no longer considers humans as a threat.

When you bring your kitten home for the first time, make sure to provide them a proper place in the house. Keep them confined in one room, to begin with, and within that room, provide them with enough toys, hiding places and various odds and ends so that it doesn't feel isolated in its confinement. Rugs, small boxes to serve as a den, an assortment of toys, and possibly a radio to filter in the occasional sounds, can serve as a primary introduction into its life with you.

Be sure to interact with them often - at least daily, but ideally more than once during a day. You have to feed them anyway, right? Give them a pet and a loving hug while you're at it, too. It may not seem like much, but it is a way for you to introduce yourselves to each other, make them feel at home, and also a continuation of the process of their socialization.

Gradually, begin to introduce him to the other members of your family. Though make sure that he has the proper vaccinations before you expose him to other cats, dogs, or other pet members in your household. Consult with your veterinarian to determine when it is safe to do so.

Don't forget that play is very important to a Calico kitten - and something that they will probably never grow out of. They enjoy playing, and thus is one very good way of socializing and bonding with them. Aside from teaching them the limits of what they can and cannot do in terms of biting and scratching, play also offers them a way to work off their high level of energy. If they don't have such an outlet, this may lead to destructive behavior later on.

Calico s are slow to mature, which they usually do when they reach three years. By then, they could go to be quite sizeable cats. There are some owners who also make it a habit of taking their cats out for a walk, and a Calico would fit a leash and harness beautifully - provided, of course, that he has been given time enough to get used to it. You will need lots of room in the house and in the backyard if you plan to keep a Calico as a pet. So while it is a good idea to fence in the yard, you could practice him for short walks on a leash out in the yard in the beginning. Later on, with your veterinarian's consent, and when you feel the cat is ready, you can begin taking him out for longer walks outside. In this way, his exposure to other places, other humans, and other dogs and cats, is supervised by you. As always, make this a positive experience for your cat, as he begins to develop his self-confidence and satisfies his natural curiosity in a safe and nurturing way.

It is not really wise to leave him to wander around like most domestic cats - regardless of whether your yard is fenced in or not. Calico s are known to be great climbers, and some are even intelligent enough to open doors and windows. You don't want him getting loose and climbing over the fence - so unless you are pretty certain of your fence, you should not leave your Calico cat outside in the yard unsupervised, or without a leash. Calico cats have a strong hunting instinct, and can literally follow their mark indefinitely. They are also extremely curious and highly energetic. Add to that the usual dangers of vehicles and roads, Calico s and the outside human world simply do not mix.

These are only rational precautions - in no time, that kitten will grow up to be a sexually mature adult, and you can never tell the degree to which it has inherited its Serval ancestor's wilder instincts. Discipline, and the limits of what he can and cannot do should be established in the beginning, during this important period of learning. Many Calico owners come to realize later on that their cats can sometimes begin behaving out of control and they can no longer rein the cats in, and they wonder what went wrong. Invest enough time, energy, patience, and training early on during the kitten's life, and you'll have a valuable Calico to keep for the rest of its life.

Litter Training for Kittens

One of the reasons why a kitten shouldn't be taken from its mother before it is ready is because kittens basically learn all that they need to know about using a litter from their mother. They emulate what they see their mother do - peeing in the box and then covering it up. Once you bring them home, half of the work should already be done. What you need to do is to make sure that this habit continues.

Below are a few tips in litter training your kitten once he comes home:

- Make sure that he is acquainted with the box. Some owners like to place him in the box directly after eating. Do this several days in a row until he gets it. He usually will get it easier than you think.
- For the first few days, keep him in a confined room that also contains the litter box. This limits his access and choices of a variety of other spots in which he can do the deed.
- Make sure that the litter box is located in a suitable spot. Don't put it near his food and water bowls, for one thing. And don't place it somewhere that is likely to be disturbed by appliances, people, or other pets. Ideally, it should be somewhere that is easily accessible by your cat, and that is at least semi-private, but not too private that it becomes difficult for you to reach and clean regularly.
- Scoop regularly. Cats are naturally fastidious creatures, and they won't appreciate having to go in an already dirty litterbox. It's akin to humans

not wanting to use a dirty toilet. It makes more work for you, but it is all part and parcel of keeping a pet in the house.

- Sometimes, cats not using the litterbox is simply a quirk of the individual cat. Vary it up, read up on what works for others, and try it out yourself. Some have reported that their cats don't like peeing and pooping in the same box, so they keep two litterboxes for their cats. Others have reported a dislike of cats sharing litter boxes with other cats, so if you keep other cats in the house, this may be it. Quite possibly, the dislike of using the litterbox may be the result of some power or dominance play between two or more cats inside the house. Sometimes, it can even be the result of an illness or condition of the bowels, and a visit to the veterinarian is in order. Or it could be the result of a changing preference in the type of litter you use. Be observant of your cat's behavior, read up, and experiment to find what works for you.

- Sometimes, what isn't working probably isn't the litterbox or litterbox habits. Some cats that feel stressed act out by not using the litter box. Look at your family's routine and how your cat is coping. Maybe he's feeling a bit stressed out or harrassed by too many changes happening within his human family.

Dealing with Problem Behaviors

If you have decided to live with a Calico , there are a few quirks of this breed that are a given, and that should be considered when you bring them home. In domestic cats, these might be considered destructive behavior, but they are simply natural for the Calico - given his high energy and wild heritage. Managing these sorts of behavioral problems probably means that you will have to adjust your lifestyle to meet their unique needs. If what you are looking for is a quiet, tame, and domestic lap cat, then the Calico cat is probably not right for you. This lovely breed needs an owner who will fully understand, accept, and know how to manage their unique quirks and traits.

- Leaving breakables out in the open is a huge no-no for a home with a Calico . And it doesn't matter how high up on the shelf you store those precious objects. These cats are climbers, and they will climb closets, shelves, trees and other high places, many times knocking over stuff to do so.
- You have to have a sense of humor when dealing with these cats. Some will hide up on a shelf and then drop things down on you when you're not looking. Others have reported their Calico s having a penchant of hiding when they're near, and then pouncing on them to scare them. They

like to play, and sometimes, they won't take no for an answer. This breed needs a lot of interaction, and the lack of an active playmate inside the home might instead lead them to some destructive behavior.

- In addition to the above, this is not a breed that you can leave alone in the house for too long. What with their need for attention, interactive game play, and their Houdini-like tactics, you might find yourself dealing with a Calico with some behavioral problems. You need to have the time and energy to devote to this breed, because this is a cat will act out, and won't respond to obvious signs of displeasure simply to please you.

- There have also been reports of aggressive Calico s that spit, hiss, and even attack people. On the one hand, this can probably be traced back to their wild Serval heritage, and the degree to which it manifests in Calico s may be affected by how far removed the cat is from its wild Serval ancestor. This is why breeders are actively trying to breed down among purebred Calico s, and outcrossing is no longer permitted. If this is your first time to bring a Calico home, opt for a later generation, ideally F4, F5 or later. On the other hand, such behavior manifesting may simply be a result of improper socialization skills when they were kittens, and not enough continuing socialization afterwards. This is why it is important to get your cat from a reputable breeder, and why prospective Calico owners should realize how much work this cat can be. One has to be willing to put in the work for this breed, and unless you are ready, willing and able to do so, then this is probably not the breed for you.

GROOMING YOUR CALICO CAT

Calico cats are generally low maintenance when it comes to grooming. But while no more than weekly grooming sessions might be needed, it is always a good idea to make each grooming session a positive experience for your Calico . Not only does it keep him clean, healthy and presentable, but positive, regular grooming sessions with you can be a wonderful bonding and socialization experience for you and your cat.

Tips for Bathing and Grooming Calico Cats

The Calico has a coat that is fairly low maintenance, with a short, soft coat that requires no more than a weekly brushing. Calico s do shed, but making coat grooming and brushing a regular thing will easily keep the likelihod of shed hair around your house under control. Remember to be gentle - especially around the belly and chest areas. Other than that, the Calico , like most fastidious cats, will pretty much take care of itself. This is also a good time for you to make a physical examination of your cat's body. Run your hands lightly around his legs, torso, neck, and back, and make sure that there aren't any abnormal lumps or swellings or other possible signs of illness or disease.

Neither will you have to bathe your cat, although some owners do begin building this habit in their kittens early on. Most of those who show their Calico s want their cat to get used to the idea of bathing, and doing it early on during the cat's life will - even if he never becomes fond of it, will at least teach him to tolerate it.

Calico s do love water, and this might make some people think that they would also love having a bath. Not necessarily - there is a big difference between liking water and being forced to submit to a bath. The Calico 's ancestor, the wild Serval, regularly hunted for frogs and small fish in water, and it is likely that your Calico may have inherited this love of water. Bathing a Calico may not be necessary, but if you do want to be able to build the habit in them, start them out when they are young. Use qualiy shampoo, and be thorough in rinsing off the shampoo from their coat. When you are only beginning, keep bath times short, and if she wants to escape from the bath, let her, and try again another time. Nothing will put a kitten off bathing more than memories of unfavorable experiences regarding the bath.

If you are one of those people, on the other hand, who are completely happy to stick to regular brushing, you might want to add some kitten wipes to your arsenal of grooming tools for cleaning the corners of your cat's eyes, their nose, and their muzzle.

Other Grooming Tasks

There are other tasks to complete your Calico 's weekly grooming, and like with coat grooming, these are also pretty straightforward. Though you might want to pay particularly close attention to your Calico 's tall ears, but aside from some extra care, cleaning their ears is not that different from how you would clean the ears of most cats.

Other grooming tasks include trimming your Calico 's nails, cleaning his ears, and brushing his teeth.

Trimming Your Cat's Nails

A cat's claws can be extra sharp - particularly if your Calico makes a regular habit of sharpening her claws. While there are some owners out there who prefer to de-claw their cat, it is generally considered more humane to simply trim their claws. Doing so weekly is a good practice.

Many cats, however, don't like it when you touch their paws, and attempting to trim their claws when they aren't used to it might cause those claws to come out! If this is your first time at trimming your cat's claws - and your cat's first time - you might want to spend a week or more just getting her used to the feeling of having her paws handled by you. You can try pressing gently on their foot to cause her to extend their claws, just to get her used to the feel of it. When you feel that you are both ready, press the paws until the claws are extended, and just snip! Use quality cat nail trimmers to do this, as using regular human nail trimmers will not work. Be conservative in the amount of nail you trim. There is a blood vessel beneath the nails that provides its blood supply, and if you aren't careful, you might end up cutting this, too.

If you aren't sure about what to do, or are nervous about wielding the nail clippers yourself, have a professional groomer or vet show you how it's done before attempting it yourself.

Cleaning Your Cat's Ears

A Calico 's ears are one of their outstanding features, and the tall pair of ears standing tall and upright also contribute to their wild look. But ears can also be a breeding ground of ear mites and other bacteria which can cause infections, so cleaning their ears is also important. But because of the sensitivity of a cat's ears -

particularly inside the ear - always remember to be gentle and careful when cleaning.

A healthy ear should be clean, with no debris, no odor, and minimal if little earwax visible. Use a moistened cotton ball or a pieze of gauze (never use q-tips!) to clean inside your cat's ears, gently wiping away any dirt or debris you find in there. Don't go too deep, or you might injure her. If you detect any bad smell or odor coming from inside their ears, then bring her immediately to a veterinarian.

Brushing Your Cat's Teeth

It may seem strange to think of brusing a cat's teeth, but cats also do suffer from some dental and oral problems like gingivitis, periodontitis, and other conditions that can affect the health of their teeth, tongue, and gums. Providing them a good chew toy can help, but it is always a good idea to build the habit of brushing their teeth early on.

Always remember to use toothbrush and toothpaste that are especially designed for cats. Using human toothpaste, for instance, is not a good idea as these contains substances that may be harmful to cats.

If you are brushing your cat's teeth for the first time, it is recommended that you first get him used to the feeling of a foreign object rubbing against his teeth. Some people may use their fingers, others use a cotton swab. Go slowly, touching only the front teeth at first by gently pushing back their lips. Use the cotton swab to gently rub it against their front teeth. Next, try dabbing some of the toothpaste on their lips. After some time, you can try applying this to your cat's teeth using the cotton swab at first, and maybe later on using a cat tootbrush.

Be patient. You might not be completely successful at first, and you'll find yourself dealing with a squirmy patient. Don't force it on your cat or you'll find him hiding from you whenever he sees you holding the toothpaste tube. Like in all matters of grooming, make it a positive experience as much as possible. With time, your Calico will get used to it, and probably even enjoy it.

BREEDING YOUR CALICO CAT

First of all, you should ask yourself why you want to breed Calico cats. If it is solely for the money - which may be tempting to some given how expensive this breed is - then this venture is probably not for you. Breeding Calico cats requires time, persistence, and a complete dedication to the development of this breed. Money itself would not be enough of a motivation to see you through the difficulties, frustrations, and years of learning that you have before you.

If, on the other hand, you are not interested in the money, and want to breed your Calico simply because you want to have their kittens, the same warnings apply. Calico s are expensive because so much goes into their breeding and development, and unless you have the proper TICA registration papers for your litter, you might have difficulty finding homes for kittens that are not registered. Already there is a growing number of unwanted Calico s out there, whether from unregistered breeders who did not know what to do with the kittens, or from owners who discovered that they no longer had the capacity to care for these energetic and lively cats.

If you are seriously considering becoming a full-pledged Calico breeder, then read on. This chapter gives a general overview of what to expect in the field of Calico cat breeding.

What It Means to Breed Calico Cats

It is important to remember that it is not legal to own Calico cats in some states in the United States. Certain states restrict ownership of Calico s, while others consider it illegal to do so. So the first thing you should do is check out the legality of owning Calico s in your area. If it is illegal where you live, that pretty much decides it for you, unless you have it in mind to move. Even if it isn't illegal, it is important to know which states restict or forbid ownership, given that you will one day be finding homes for the kittens. Breeding responsibly means taking care of your kittens from birth until they find new and loving homes.

Calico cats are a relatively new breed, and they were only accepted for Championship Status by TICA in 2012. TICA is the only cat organization in the world that recognizes and accepts this hybrid breed, and even now, Calico s can only be shown in the Advanced New Breed category because there are, as yet, not enough registered cats to warrant showing in the Championship category.

And because this breed is, in many ways, still not firmly established, breeders can get pretty technical when it comes to Calico breeding lingo and expertise. Below you will find some of the more common terminologies you will come across sooner or later when you are dealing with Calico cats, followed by some of the difficulties inherent in Calico cat breeding.

Filial Generation: (F1, F2, F3, etc.)

"Filial" refers to family generation, and this is reckoned from how far away an offspring is from its Serval ancestor. The offspring of a Serval and a domestic cat is referred to as "F1" - as in the case of the original Calico cat produced by the crossbreeding of an African Serval and a domestic Siamese cat.

An F2 generation has the Serval for a grandparent, or is two generations away. An F3 has a great grandparent who is a Serval, and so on. The filial generation reckoned by numbers tells you how far away a Calico is down the line from a wild African Serval cat.

"A-Registered", "B-Registered," "C-Registered" or "SBT"

Calico s are also distinguised based on their level of Calico breeding - which is what the TICA uses for the registration of Calico cats. The above are the Registration Codes that TICA uses in its Feline Registry.

For instance, "A-Registered Calico s" are those with one Calico parent - usually the result of an outcross with one of the permissible outcross breeds - e.g., a Calico and a Domestic Shorthair.

"B-Registered Calico s" mean that the cat has two Calico parents, but not all grandparents are Calico s. So if you cross two "A-Registered" Calico s, or if you cross one "A-Registered Calico " and one "B-Registered Calico , you will get a "B-Registered Calico " because even if both parents are Calico s, the cat still has one outcross grandparent.

"C-Registered Calico s" mean that both parents and all four grandparents are Calico s. "C-Registered" Calico s are the result of two generations of Calico to Calico breeding, with no outcrosses in those two generations. Crossing two "B-Registered," or crossing one "B-Registered" and one "C-Registered" Calico will result in a "C-Registered" Calico .

"SBT," which stands for "Stud Book Traditional," means that the Calico is the result of three generations of Calico -to-Calico breeding. Crossing two "C-Registered" Calico s will result in an SBT, and they are what the TICA considers "purebred" Calico s. Any serious Calico cat breeder should aim for the production of SBT Calico s, and as more SBT cats are bred, it is hoped the Calico s will become more established as a breed.

Difficulties Inherent in Calico Cat Breeding

There are a few inherent difficulties in Calico cat breeding, and it takes patience, dedication, and a good working knowledge of feline crossbreeding to hurdle these difficulties. The list below is by no means exhaustive, neither is it certain in all instances and situations. But they should put prospective breeders on the alert as to the roadblocks that may lie ahead of them as they seek to contribute in the development of the Calico cat breed.

- Calico cat ownership is restricted in some states in the United States, and illegal in others. You need to do your background check on local ordinances and laws governing the legality of wild or domesticated hybrid crosses in your area, and definitely regarding licensing laws before you even consider starting a breeding program. Outside of the United States, Canada has certain restrictions on the ownership of F1 and F2 generations, and special permits are required for importing these cats from the United States. In Australia, importation of the Calico cat is banned.

- While you are essentially "breeding down" a wild cat - keeping their wild appearance as much as possible while retaining the temperaments of more domestic cats, you cannot completely get rid of their wild nature. These are energetic cats, great jumpers and climbers, and there have been reports of some Calico s intelligent enough to open drawers, closet doors, and even windows. They will spray to mark their territory, and some have even been reported to hunt local wildlife and other smaller pets in the nearby areas. You need a good and secure area for a cattery, and you will need to be able to maintain some semblance of discipline among the Calico s you will be housing. Traits of the wild Serval are usually more pronounced among the earlier Calico generations. Daily, regular and constant socialization and supervision is a must to prevent them from reverting to the wild. It goes without saying that cruelty, neglect and abandonment are not options once you discover that these cats are a handful for you - better know what you're getting into before bringing one of these cats home, or before you start a breeding program.

- Male fertility seems to be a problem among the earlier generations of Calico s - one of the more common manifestations of hybrid inviability. Male Calico s are usually sterile until the fifth generation and later, and even F5 males are usually smaller than the females, which makes breeding difficult. Recently, sterile male Calico s have also appeared in F5 to F6 generations. You will usually have to breed fertile F5 or later generation males to earlier generations of females - all of which are usually fertile. And because earlier generation females are usually larger in size than their male counterparts, this also provides some difficulties in the actual breeding process.

- In order to retain the desirable characteristics of the "purebred" Calico - you will have to be selective about the cats you breed. Remember that what you are aiming for are the clear, spotted coat patterns and other physical characteristics set out in the TICA Breed Standard, but with a friendly temperament that is closer to its domestic, rather than its wild, ancestry. In order to achieve this desirable traits, outcrosses were permitted to selected breeds, including: Oriental Shorthairs, Egyptian Maus, Ocicat, and the Domestic Shorthair. TICA considers the following as "impermissible" outcrosses: Bengal and Maine Coon cats. These days, however, outcrossing is seldom used as there are now enough male Calico studs available. Regardless, however, you still have to aim to breed for the desirable traits, avoiding genetic illnesses and genetic and temperamental "flaws" as much as possible.

- Pregnancies that result from crossbreeding are often difficult. Because of the differences in size between the parents (even among Calico -to-Calico breeding, where the sizes can vary greatly even in one litter), and the difference in gestation period between domestic cats and Servals, some kittens may be born prematurely and then require round-the-clock care. In some instances, pregnancies are either aborted or absorbed.

- Serval females are picky about their mates, and this characteristic also seems to appear in the earlier generations of Calico females - which are usually larger compared to later generations. While crossbreeding does happen, even among hybrid Calico s, it may be quite difficult to produce a successful mating or breeding between a larger female Calico and a smaller male Calico or smaller male domestic cat, especially when the female is uncooperative.

As a final word, you should seek registration with TICA as a Calico cat breeder if you are really serious about breeding these gorgeous cats. You will generally be required to sign the TICA Code of Ethics, submit the required forms and pay the requisite fees, and be familiar with the By-laws, Registration Rules, Show Rules and Standing Laws of TICA. This registration needs to be renewed annually. Active membership and participation can provide the breeder with an extensive network of fellow breeders and Calico cat enthusiasts to network with, exchange ideas with, have a discussion or conversation with, and just to share their love for and commitment to the development of the Calico breed.

Basic Cat Breeding Information

Breeding Calico s is generally no different from breeding most cats, except for a few crucial provisos:

- Breeding a larger Calico with a domestic cat can be difficult - not only because of their size differences, but also because of the difference in their instinctive temperaments. In some instances, some female Calico s will not willingly mate with a domestic cat - their female Serval ancestor usually chooses her mate in the wild. In other instances, breeding a Calico and a smaller domestic cat can actually result in the injury, and sometimes even the death, of the smaller domestic cat. Keep in mind that when you are breeding cats with wild ancestry, constant supervision is necessary when they are brought together with other smaller pets and animals.

- Secondly, the gestation period between a domestic cat and a wild cat is different, which can make for a difficult pregnancy. 65 days is the average gestation period for a domestic cat, while it is 75 days for a Serval. When you cross the two, or cross any of their offspring, some of the difficulties involved include pregnancies that are absorbed, aborted, or kittens that are born prematurely.

- It is generally advised that a prospective Calico cat breeder begin with Calico cats as their foundation breed. The original ancestors of the Calico included the wild African Serval, but unless you have the knowledge, the capacity and the experience in dealing with wild cats, bringing one into your cattery is not recommended. Nor is crossing your Calico with another hybrid wild cat such as the Bengal. If you really want to breed Calico s, breed from the many later generations of Calico s that have been produced. The TICA-stated goal is to achieve purebred Calico s which are the result of at least three generations of Calico to Calico breeding.

Despite all the above-noted possible difficulties, Calico breeding proceeds along the same general lines as the breeding process of most other breeds. Regardless of whether or not you aim to breed your Calico , one of the first things you should be familiar with is the feline heat cycle. If you don't intend to breed your cat, then do the responsible thing and have him or her neutered. Doing so before they reach puberty or sexual maturity will not only reduce the risk of mammary cancer among the females, it will also prevent some of the more aggressive, sex-related behaviors such as yowling (calling), and among males - spraying or marking territory, and aggression.

The Feline Heat Cycle

In general, female cats reach their age of first heat at around 6 months, sometimes earlier at about 4-5 months. Male cats become sexually mature at around the same time, or about 5-7 months. Most breeders, however, do not recommend mating or breeding a cat at their age of first heat, but 18-24 months old or later, if possible. It is always advisable to wait until the cat has enough maturity and is fully grown before she bears the responsibility and stress of pregnancy and motherhood. In the meantime, it is incumbent upon the breeder to control or manage the female's heat cycles.

Cats are seasonally polyestrous, which means that they can be in heat several times during a year. And since males are typically attracted to a female cat in heat, unintentional or accidental matings may occur - which you don't want to happen, especially for a wild hybrid breed like the Calico , unless you are willing to take responsibility for her kittens. A female cat can mate with multiple males while in heat, and because they are induced ovulators, they can produce a litter that has been sired by different cats, which is also known as superfecundity. It is estimated that a single cat can produce two to three litters per year, or up to 150 kittens in their breeding span of about ten years. This is why it is essential to know how to manage a female cat in heat. Not only will multiple pregnancies and births task the health of your queen, there is also the problem of the kittens and finding homes for all of them. Cat overpopulation is already a global problem. Some breeders choose to alternate breeding every two or three heat cycles, and then having the queen spayed when she reaches 5-6 years of age.

Be discerning in your selection of the queen and stud - not only should they be perfectly healthy and of the proper age, but you should also make your selection based on the ideal temperament of the kittens you are breeding. Many Calico cats still do retain some of the wilder instincts of their Serval ancestors, which makes them difficult to care for especially when they grow old.

A cat's heat cycle moves in stages, the first of which is proestrus, which can last from 1-2 days, or sometimes even less. During proestrus, she will be "calling," and while she will not be willing to mate just yet, she will show some distinctive behaviors such as rolling around on the floor, licking her genitals, rubbing against your legs or against furniture, and she will have a propensity to try to escape the house in her attempts to find a mate.

During the second stage, or estrus, the queen will be ready to mate. It is advisable to keep your stud and queen together during this time to allow for repeated or multiple matings and a successful pregnancy. Chances are, she will get pregnant from the later matings, after she has already been induced to ovulate. You don't want another tomcat sneaking in in the meantime and fathering a few kittens. On the average, estrus can last for about a week, though sometimes for a shorter or longer period depending on the cat.

A female cat that has not been bred during estrus will enter the interestrus stage, which lasts for about a week, after which she will again start her cycle, entering the proestrus and estrus stages once more. If a queen has not been bred for successive heat cycles, then her cycles will become longer and more frequent. It is generally not advisable to allow three heat cycles to go by without breeding, so breeders usually seek to manage their cat's cycle in various ways. Consult your veterinarian for help in managing your queen's heat cycle.

If your cat was bred and ovulated, but she did not become pregnant, she enters metestrus, during which she will not show any signs of reproductive activity or about 5-7 weeks. If, on the other hand, the breeding was successful, she will enter a gestation period lasting for an average of 65-77 days. If the queen aborts or loses her kittens for whatever reason, she will once again resume her cycle after about 2-3 weeks.

Pregnancy and Queening

A pregnant or nursing mother is referred to as queen, and the process of birthing is referred to as queening. Some of the signs of a pregnant queen are nipples that are enlarged and more pink, weight gain, and a noticeable increase in appetite. You probably won't be able to tell that your cat is pregnant until she is sometime in her third week of pregnancy, which can be confirmed by a veterinarian. Around two weeks before she is due, you'll find her becoming more affectionate, and definite signs of nesting behavior such as seeking out solitary or private areas. Consult with your veterinarian regarding dietary changes, but in general, it is advisable to gradually increase your cat's diet during the final weeks of gestation until she is eating about 25% of her usual diet. This increased food intake will have to be kept up until after she has given birth and is lactating, to help her produce enough milk as she nurses her kittens.

Cats in general including Calico cats, don't usually require much assistance during the birthing process, or during queening. What you can do is prepare a nesting box for her that should be large enough to contain both the mother and her kittens. This should be placed in a private room that is not often disturbed by pet or human traffic, or other loud noises or sounds. You should introduce her to this box, get her comfortable with it for the few weeks before she is due, and chances are she will give birth in that nesting box. Though be prepared for the possibility that she might want to sneak off somewhere when you aren't looking and have her kittens somewhere more secret. Sometimes, she'll probably surprise you one morning when you wake up and she has already given birth to her litter. Follow her and make sure that her choice of a birthing site is safe and secure, moving the kittens to the box if possible, with as little time as you can manage spent holding each kitten. Too much human handling early on may cause the mother to reject a kitten. If she was amenable enough to have her litter in the box you provided, be sure you are there with her when she does give birth, ready to provide assistance should it be necessary. Have the number of your vet and local emergency services on hand in case there is trouble, and if this is your first time, it is always advisable to have an experienced breeder with you to help and guide you through the process. In general, though, most cats will give birth without any help, their instincts kicking in quite strongly even for first time mothers.

The average size of a Calico litter is variable, though it can range anywhere from 1 to 5 kittens. Their size will also vary, depending on the generation. Sometimes kittens of the same litter will also vary in size. Much of these details will depend on the breeding program you are adopting, and which Calico generation you are breeding.

Make sure that the queen is nursing all her kittens. Some breeders advise leaving the kittens alone to bond with the queen for at least the first two days. Just ensure that they are kept warm and away from cold spots or chills. After this, it is time to gradually begin the process of socialization - even if it is only just regular momentary handling of the kittens in the beginning. Be gentle and careful in handling the kittens, and try to maintain the same level of attention and care for the pregnant queen as she nurses her kittens. Consult with your veterinarian regarding the best dietary plan for your new mother.

Raising and Weaning Kittens

TICA has advised that there is no real need to treat Calico s differently than domestic cats when it comes to the food they eat, and most can be weaned the same way, too - through a gradual transition to moistened cat food until they no longer need to nurse from their mother. Some recommend using the kitten food you are aiming to feed them later on, moistened with formula.

Weaning usually begins at about 4 weeks, when the kittens start trying to eat their mother's food. Normally, the mother will push away the kittens. To begin the weaning process, you can try smearing the formula around the kittens' mouths at first, which they will eventually lick off. Once they have gotten used to the taste of the food, you can begin providing this to them in bowls. At the same time that you are gradually increasing the food intake of the kittens, you can also begin decreasing their mother's food intake to help her milk dry up naturally.

In general, most kittens are fully weaned by around 8-12 weeks, but this can be variable, and some Calico kittens might require a longer period of time before they are fully weaned and ready to be separated from their mother. Don't rush it. As much as possible, kittens should not be rushed or forced or it might lead to potentially destructive behavior later on.

SHOWING YOUR CALICO CAT

If you are thinking of or planning on joining or entering your Calico cat in a show, then this chapter is for you. At present, there is only one cat organization that registers Calico cats - and that is the same organization which has figured so prominently in the history of this new breed's recognition and acceptance. The International Cat Association, or TICA, is currently the only cat organization that recognizes the Calico cat breed, which they have granted Championship Status in 2012.

If you want to show your Calico cat, therefore, the first thing you should do is familiarize yourself with TICA's published breed standard for the Calico cat breed, and also with TICA's rules and regulations, and the requirements on how to register and join.

Calico Cat Breed Standard

Calico s were granted championship status by TICA in 2012, but with a few provisos. Any Calico cat joining a cat show must be at least four months or age, is at least an F3 or further generation from the Serval, and must be of any of the permissible colors: Black Spotted Tabby (BST), Silver Spotted Tabby (SST), black, or smoke. In addition, the Calico must be a C or SBT registered cat. This registration terminology means:

- "C" registered cats are the result of two "B" registered Calico s. For "C" registered Calico s, both the parents and the grandparents are Calico s, but at least one grandparent is of a different breed.
- "B" registered Calico s are the result of the cross between two "A" registered Calico s. "B" registered Calico s have both parents that are Calico s, but at least one grandparent of a different breed.
- "A" registered Calico s simply means that one parent is not a Calico .
- When you cross two "C" registered Calico s, what you have is an SBT, which stands for "Stud Book Traditional." This means that there are three generations of Calico to Calico breeding in the cat's ancestry - the parents, the grandparents, and the great-grandparents.

"SBT"s are what are considered by TICA as "purebred" cats.

At present, Calico s are being shown at the Advanced New Breed status. Only when enough SBT kittens are registered will Calico s be moved to the Championship status, and "C" kittens will no longer be allowed to be shown. When this happens, only SBT Calico s, or purebred Calico s, will be shown.

Below is a summary of TICA's published Breed Standard for the Calico Cat Breed.

General

The Calico is tall, lean, and graceful, with striking dark spots and other bold markings on a background color of any shade of brown, silver, black, or black smoke. They closely resemble the African Serval, but are smaller in stature. They are affectionate, outgoing, with a long neck, long legs, tall ears, and a medium length tail.

Head, Chin, Nose, Muzzle and Neck

The face forms an equilateral triangle which is formed by the brow line, the sides following the jaw bone, and a rounded finish at the muzzle. Above this the forehead from the brow line and the tops of the ears form a rectangle. The head is small in proportion to the body.

The chin tapers to follow the triangle of the head; in profile, the nose protrudes slightly so the chin may appear recessed.

The nose is wide across the top, with low set nostrils. In profile, there is a slight downward turn at the end, giving a rounded appearance. The nose leather is slightly convex and wraps up over the nose.

The muzzle is tapered with no break. Whisker pads are not pronounced.

The neck is long and lean.

Ears

The ears are large and high on the head, wide and with a deep base. These are very upright and with rounded tops. Ideally, a vertical line can be drawn from the inner corner of the eye to the inner base of the ear. Ear furnishings may be present, pronounced ocelli (spots on the backs of the ears, or "eyes on the back of the head") are considered desirable.

Eyes

The eyes are medium in size, set underneath a slightly hooded brow. The top resembles a boomerang, set at an angle so that the corner slopes down the line of the nose. The bottom half of the eye has an almond shape. The eyes are low on the forehead, at least one eye's width apart. All eye colors are allowed and are independent of coat color.

Boning and Musculature

The boning is medium in density and strength.

The musculature is firm, well-developed, but smooth.

Coat, Coat Colors and Coat Patterns

The coat is short to medium in length, of good substance and with a slightly coarse feel. Coarser guard hairs cover a softer undercoat, and the spots are notably softer in texture than the guard hairs. The coat lies relatively flat against the body.

Acceptable coat colors are either solid, tabby, or silver/smoke, in colors ranging from black, brown (black), spotted tabby, black silver spotted tabby, and black smoke.

For black Calico s, the nose leather must be solid black. Bold, solid markings are preferred in all tabbies, and in any variation, the lips are black, and tear duct lines are prominent. For spotted Calico s, the nose leather can be pink to brick red, surrounded by a line, solid black, or black with a pink to brick center stripe. In either color variation, the paw pads are either deep charcoal or brownish black.

Only spotted patterns are accepted: either solid dark-brown or black spots, whether round, oval, or elongated. A series of parallel stripes run from the back of the head to just over the shoulder blades, fanning out slightly over the back. The spotting pattern follows the line of the stripes, with smaller spots on the legs and feet, as well as on the face.

For black Calico s, ghost spotting may occur. For smoke Calico s, a visible spotting pattern is preferred.

Temperament

The Calico is confident, alert, curious, and friendly.

Disqualifications

Calico s with extra toes are disqualified.

Any sign of challenge in temperament shall disqualify.

Registering Your Calico with TICA

Because of the recent development of this hybrid breed, documentation and registration of Calico s have been fairly easy and straightforward. Registered Calico breeders are expected to register their cats or their kitten litters with TICA. This means that when you purchased your Calico , either your cat must have already been registered, or you will receive a "blue slip" together with your kitten upon purchase. This blue slip is the breeder's litter registration form, which you can use to register your Calico with TICA. If already registered, the breeder will sign over the registration papers to you, which you will also need to send off to TICA. In both instances, you will need to pay a small fee. Take note that if they come in the "non-standard" colors or coat patterns, you can still register them, though you may not be able to show them.

Preparing Your Calico Cat for Show

The preparation of your Calico for show must have already started long before the date of the show itself, ideally as kittens. First of all, any Calico owner desiring to show their cat in a TICA show must make sure that their cat falls squarely within the classifications of acceptable Calico s: either an F3 or later generation, a "C" or "SBT" registered cat, and possesses the acceptable coat colors and patterns of TICA. It might happen, therefore, that either you wished to show Calico cats even when you purchased your kitten, and therefore looked for kittens that fell squarely under TICA's category of acceptable Calico s for show, or you had no notion of showing when you purchased your kitten, but have been gratified later on to learn that your Calico is acceptable for show on all points. Either way, preparing your Calico for show must have started long before the show itself.

The preparation process itself is not different from preparing many other breeds of cats:

- A continuous socialization process ideally begun as kittens, so that your cat is not spooked, threatened, shy or timid around humans. Your Calico will be handled by the judges during the show, so it is recommended that you get them used to being handled by several different people - in the same way that judges also handle show cats. A visit to a cat show will be very instructive.

- Steady nurturing and care in terms of health, diet, nutrition, and grooming. How healthy and how well-groomed your cat is during the show itself is the result of a lifetime of work: from careful attention to their diet and nutrition, regular veterinary and health checks, and regular and careful grooming. Grooming involves trimming nails, cleaning ears, regular brushing, brushing their teeth, and even bathing. Most show cats are, in fact, bathed prior to the date of the show itself (either a day or several days before the show), and you can only do this effectively if bathing is a habit that has been built over the cat's lifetime.

- Near the date of the show, you must already have learned the Breed Show standard by heart. This is because cat shows are not precisely a competition between cats to show which cat or cat breed is best. Cat shows aim to showcase cats that are the best or strong examples of their breed standards. And different breeds have different standards. How strong an example of the Breed Standard is your Calico ?

The next thing for you to do is gather relevant information: the schedules, dates and venues of the nearest TICA cat show, and the rules and regulations of TICA governing cat shows. Researching these should be fairly easy as there are a lot of informative guides on TICA's website. Some of TICA's show rules include:

- declawed cats shall not be penalized
- each entry should have its claws clipped prior to benching
- obviously pregnant cats or kittens are ineligible
- each cat has a single benching cage. Double cages and grooming spaces are available at additional cost

You might also want to pay a visit to one or more of these shows beforehand, just to see how things are conducted. Take note that Calico s cannot be shown in the Household Pet (HHP) category, as New Trait or New Breeds are not allowed in HHPs.

When you're ready, here is a general procedure on how to join your first cat show:

- Check the nearest TICA show, the date, venue and requirements. Obtain an entry form, fill it in, and submit it together with the requisite fees.
- You will be receiving a confirmation. Check this carefully, and report any errors immediately prior to the event.
- Upon arrival at the show, your cat may be checked by a vet to confirm that it is not suffering from any illness, and has no signs of parasites such as mites, fleas, or fungal infections.
- You will be asked to show the confirmation papers, as well as a current vaccination certificate, so be sure to prepare these beforehand.

It is recommended that you arrive early as check-in lines can sometimes be quite long. Once you have finished checking in, you should proceed to the designated area where your cat is benched. You should begin setting up your cage curtains, the litter pan, and water dishes. Cage curtains are considered important as these gives your cat privacy. These may be simple or elaborate depending on your taste, as long as it fits the back, sides and top of the cage. Once you have finished setting up, relax, and enjoy the show.

You will probably not be able to leave the show while it is still ongoing, so here is a general checklist of things you should prepare beforehand to bring with you:

- cage curtains and clips
- litter and litter box
- food and water bowls
- nail clippers
- grooming equipment
- confirmation receipt
- vaccination records
- registration papers

KEEPING YOUR CALICO CAT HEALTHY

The general consensus is that Calico cats are one of the healthiest and hardiest breed of felines. To date, they have no known breed-specific problems. But this is not a guarantee of absolute good health. They can still be prone to many of the deady diseases afflicting the feline population, and for which they should receive the appropriate vaccinations, if available.

And because the development of the Calico cats as a hybrid breed is fairly recent - it will take more time before experts can agree on what are or are not breed-specific health conditions among Calico s. That said, there are a few health conditions that have appeared in some Calico s, and which Calico owners should be on the alert for.

Potential Health Problems Affecting Calico Cats

Like most other cats, Calico s should be screened before breeding to rule out potential incidences of hereditary and non-hereditary health conditions. There have been certain incidences of Calico cats being diagnosed with the following conditions, though their prevalence in the breed as a whole has not yet been fully determined.

Some of the potential health conditions that may affect Calico cats include:

- Hypertrophic Cardiomyopathy (HCM)
- Pyruvate Kinase (PK) Deficiency
- Taurine Deficiency

Hypertrophic Cardiomyopathy (HCM)

Hypertrophic Cardiomyopathy (HCM) is the most common heart disease seen in cats. This is a genetic condition, and is a concern among many purebreed cats. Cases of HCM have been found in some Calico s, and it is recommended that breeders screen their breeder cats annually for HCM.

In some cats, there are no distinctive clinical signs of HCM, and the difficulty is that because it occurs more commonly among cats 5-7 years of age, it can only manifest itself after a cat has been bred. And since HCM can also manifest even after testing, annual screening important.

Some of the signs and symptoms to watch out for include:

- labored or rapid breathing

- lethargy
- open-mouthed breathing
- loss of appetite
- abnormal heart sounds or heart murmurs
- inability to tolerate exercise or exertion
- hind limb paralysis or signs of acute pain in the hind limbs
- sudden collapse

The variation in symptoms is caused by the varying effect of the thickening in the heart. Accumulation of fluid in or near the lungs can cause breathing or respiratory difficulties. Thromboembolism is caused by the development of a clot in the heart that when ejected into the system, can lodge in the periphery like the legs. This is what can cause pain or paralysis in the hind legs. And finally, the abnormal blood flow causes distinctive heart murmurs or abnormal heart rhythm.

Diagnosis is done through an echocardiograph or ultrasound imaging, which allows for a visual examination of the heart for signs of enlargement or thickening of the walls. This is currently the best method available for detecting HCM. Other possible diagnostic tools available is an electrocardiogram (EKG) and a Radiography (X-rays). A diagnosis of HCM can be made after ruling out hypertension and hyperthyroidism, which conditions can cause the same or similar symptoms.

There are medications available for HCM, depending on the severity and the symptoms.

- Beta-blockers for slowing down the heart rate
- Calcium-channel blockers for reducing the heart rate and contractions.
- ACE-inhibitors for congestive heart failure
- Aspirin and Warfarin to reduce the risk of blood clots
- Diuretics to remove excess fluid from the body
- Nitroglycerine ointment to dilate the vein and arteries

In severe cases, your cat may need to be hospitalized, kept in a stress-free environment and undergo oxygen therapy for difficulties in breathing.

Other things that you can do at home for your cat is to keep the environment safe and stress-free for your Calico , restrict their sodium intake, and make sure that they avoid getting cold or chilled. Keep them in a reasonably warm room at all times. Make sure that they are brought to the vet at least every 6 months so that his condition can be monitored and any medication he is taking can be adjusted accordingly.

The prognosis of Calico s diagnosed with HCM varies, as many of those with HCM may never develop any of the outward or clinical symptoms. On the other hand, congestive heart failure, thromboembolism, and hypothermia can signal poor prognosis, and may significantly decrease a cat's life span.

Pyruvate Kinase (PK) Deficiency or PKD

PK Deficiency is essentially an inherited condition in which the enzyme Pyruvate Kinase (PK) is missing or lacking. This enzyme is important for red blood cell energy metabolism, and its lack can lead to the instability and loss of red blood cells. Essentially, PK Deficiency is an inherited form of hemolytic anemia.

The onset of this condition is variable, and can manifest at any age. The symptoms are also variable, but can include severe lethargy, weakness, jaundice, weight loss, and abdominal enlargement. The severity of this condition can also vary, appearing as a mild and intermittent condition in some, but rapid and life-threatening in others.

There is a DNA test available to screen for this condition, and any prospective Calico breeding cat must be screened for PK Deficiency. Depending on whether one or both parents are affected or are carriers, the offspring can also be carriers or be affected. This test is generally done by a simple mouth swab and the sample sent for laboratory analysis. In the results, your cat can either be clean, a carrier, or positive for PK Deficiency.

If positive, all is not necessarily lost. Some PK Deficiency positive cats can still live through its normal life span, showing only occasional signs of lethargy and anemia. It is a good idea to bring your cat to the vet so that you can map out potential medical treatment and and a rehabilitation plan, including lifestyle (diet and exercise) choices to address the symptoms. Needless to say, breeding from PK Deficiency-positive Calico s is not recommended. In fact it is probably a good idea to inform the breeder from whom you have purchased your Calico about the DNA results so that breeding from your cat's parents can also be discontinued - depending on whether one or both were carriers or affected.

Carrier cats are not likely to display any of the clinical signs of PK Deficiency, but it is a good idea to have them tested anyway. If they are confirmed carriers, breeding from them is also not advised - especially if they are paired with another carrier or another affected parent cat. There is still a chance that the condition might be carried on down the line. Being carrier, they can still live a long, happy, and healthy life - though of course they should no longer be included in breeding programs.

Taurine Deficiency

Calico cats may be prone to Taurine Deficiency. This seems to be a nutritional inadequacy, and may be addressed quite effectively through diet and supplements, especially with kittens that are still in their developmental stages. Early on, particular attention should be paid to a Calico cat's diet to guard against Taurine Deficiency.

Taurine is an amino acid that can be found in meats and fish, particularly in hearts and livers. High concentrations of Taurine can be found in meat, poultry, fish, and premium cat foods. They could not be found in vegetables, so feeding your Calico a meat-based diet, or a meat-based cat food, is essential. It is theorized that the diet of cats in the wild - particularly the Calico 's ancestor, the Serval - is comprised, in a large part, by rodents. Servals were able to get all the Taurine that they needed from these rodents - whose brains were rich with this amino acid. While most cats require significant levels of Taurine in their diet, this may be a particular need for Calico s due to the close proximity of their Serval heritage. At least, most breeders seem to agree that the Calico 's need for Taurine is greater than most other cats.

Taurine should be provided significantly in your Calico 's diet because cats, unlike other animals, derive their Taurine mostly from their diet. Cats cannot make enough Taurine internally for their needs, and if domesticated cats do not get enough Taurine from the food we feed them, Taurine Deficiency is almost always a certainty. In the 1970s, it was proven that many of the commercial cat foods at the time lacked sufficient Taurine, after many of the symptoms of Taurine Deficiency began appearing among domestic cats. Most major cat foods revised their formula to meet this need, but the difficulty is that some breeds seem to require more Taurine than others, and not all Taurine provides the same nutritional value. Some forms may be needed to be provided in larger volume for proper utilization and absorption by felines.

Taurine is an important nutritional need for cats. Among its uses are:

- it prevents dilated cardiomyopathy, or the failure of the heart muscle, or the inability of the heart muscle to meet the body's circulatory needs, thus swelling in the process

- promotes intestinal absorption of lipids (fats) as cholesterol
- prevents Feline Central Retinal Degeneration (FCRD), which is a progressive retinal disease among cats
- assists in reproductive processes, prevending incidence of still births, fewer than normal kittens, or fewer surviving kittens.

Some of the symptoms of Taurine Deficiency include:

- stunted growth
- the development of cardiomyopathy
- bones that do not develop properly
- loss of hair
- loss of teeth or tooth decay
- Taurine Deficiency in queens might produce kittens that are deformed or who die soon after birth; she may also produce a smaller litter than average, smaller-size kittens than average, or she might even inadvertently abort her fetuses
- Taurine Deficiency might also cause eye problems and irreversible blindness (Central Retinal Degeneration or CRD)

You can provide sufficient levels of Taurine to your cat through meats or meat-based diets or meat-based cat food, or additionally through supplements. Consult with your veterinarian to determine recommended amounts of Taurine for your Calico kitten or cat, as dietary prescriptions and nutritional supplements should never be attempted without proper consultation and advice from your Vet.

Smaller Livers and Ketamine

Some veterinarians have noted that some Calico s have inherited from Servals the tendency to have smaller livers relative to their body sizes. The precise medical effects of this has not yet been fully determined.

Some are of the opinion that greater care should be taken in the administration of medication such as the anesthetic Ketamine, which needs to be metabolized by the liver. Ketamine is often used in surgical procedures, and if your Vet is not familiar with the particular needs of Calico s, breeders advise that you request that Isoflourine gas be used instead, or an injectable anesthetic protocol specific to exotic or hybrid bred felines. Using Ketamine, some breeders claim, may have potential ill effects that may sometimes even be lethal.

By contrast, many veterinarians are of the opinion that there is no particular difference between hybrid cats and other domestic cats that warrant different medical treatments, such as specific requirements in the use of anesthetic agents like Ketamine. Ketamine as an anesthetic cannot be used alone, and so perhaps the current opinion among many breeders of the dangers posed by Ketamine to Calico s may have resulted from a misunderstanding of the drug and its administration. After all, they argue that Ketamine, used in servals and together with other specific elements, has already been proven safe.

The reader here is advised that while opinions on both sides are strong, there is no definitive proof either way. It is up to you to determine the particular needs of your Calico , and if you feel that taking the safer route by avoiding Ketamine is preferred, you can certainly make this request of your vet. Perhaps it is best to seek out a veterinarian who specializes in, or has had some experience with hybrid breeds to begin with. Just make sure that any choice you make is an informed one, and is one that you are fully comfortable with.

Preventing Illness with Vaccinations

There has been much controversy regarding the do's and don't's of pet vaccinations in recent years, and many have held to strong but differing opinions. For a novice cat owner, it is difficult to sift through much of the recent debates, contrasting information, and strong sentiments from both pet owners and the veterinary community. How do you know which is which? Some pet owners who have seen for themselves the ill effects (or absence of ill effects) of vaccinations will have solid experience to back up their future judgments. But what about one who is bringing home a Calico kitten for the first time?

In addition, there has been widespread opinion among Calico breeders that Calico cats should only be given killed vaccines, and never modified-live. There is also an addendum that Calico s should not be vaccinated for FeLV (Feline Leukemia Virus) and FIP (Feline Infectious Peritonitus). These are based on reports of alleged bad side effects among Calico s, and in the case of modified live vaccines, may even predispose the cat to contract the very disease they are being vaccinated against.

We say "alleged" because there have so far been no documented case or scientific finding to bolster these claims. And yet it might not cause any harm to take the safe and cautious route in such a volatile and confusing area of cat health care. Aside from the above precautions which Calico breeders state are necessary, there does not seem to be any other differences between vaccination requirements of Calico cats and other cat breeds.

If you are worried about the different advise, recommendations and opinions regarding vaccinations, the best thing to do is to sit down and have a conversation with your veterinarian. Most vaccination schedules - including the frequency of booster shots - will have to be adjusted anyway depending on your unique needs: your cat's state of health, age, lifestyle, medical history, state-required vaccines, and whether or not there are diseases currently prevalent and therefore threatening in your area or region. Don't hesitate to ask questions if there are things you don't understand, or if you have any doubts or worries.

As we proceed with this section on vaccinations, please take note that we are only providing general guidelines that are applicable to cats in general. The specific vaccines your cat will receive, and their frequency, will always vary depending on your unique circumstances. Don't forget that vaccines were developed to protect your cat's health, and have in fact saved many cats from what were once deadly and lethal diseases among the feline population.

Core Vaccines

Core vaccines are precisely what their name implies: necessary and obligatory vaccines for all cats, regardless of individual circumstances. They are designed to protect your cat from lethal diseases that are globally prevalent among cats.

The following are considered core vaccines:

- Rabies
- Feline viral Rhinotracheitis (FVR), also known as feline influenza
- Feline Calcivirus (FCV)
- Feline Panleukopenia Virus (FPV), also known as feline distemper

Non Core Vaccines

Non-core vaccines, on the other hand, are vaccines administered only depending upon need: whether or not the region, the lifestyle, or the local environment places the cat in greater risk of contracting any of the following:

- Chlamydophila felis

- Feline Leukemia Virus (FeLV)
- Feline Immunodeficiency Virus (FIV)
- Bordetella

Please take note that the following vaccines are **not** recommended in all circumstances. There is no evidence of their effectiveness, and an equally high possibility of adverse reactions.

- Feline Infectious Peritonitis (FIP)
- Giardia Lamblia

The table below shows a general schedule of vaccinations for kittens. Non-core vaccinations may be recommended based on the region where you lived and the risk of exposure. Core vaccinations will need to be boostered after a year, and then either one to three years afterwards, depending on the vaccine used.

CPSIA information can be obtained
at www.ICGtesting.com
Printed in the USA
LVHW050114110122
708206LV00016B/2383